The JOY of RELATIONSHIP

The JOY of RELATIONSHIP

Robert E. Fisher

Pathway PRESS

CLEVELAND, TENNESSEE

Library of Congress Catalog Card Number: 97-065158
ISBN: 871484544
Copyright © 1997 by Pathway Press
Cleveland, Tennessee 37311
All Rights Reserved
Printed in the United States of America

Because they
symbolize in so
many joyful ways
the fulfillment of God's
promise to me, this book
is dedicated to my six
wonderful grandchildren:
Emily, Matthew, Grant,
David, Amanda and
Mallory.

Yea, thou shalt see
thy children's children...
Psalm 128:6

CONTENTS

FOREWORD

Already a best-selling author that has blessed thousands of readers with his insightful studies of love, devotion and other spiritual requisites, Robert E. Fisher now surveys the gamut of emotions and attitudes that distinguish a balanced Christian life, and examines the important corrections that occur during a lifetime—those with God, with others, and with oneself. As this book makes abundantly clear, our life relationships are as diverse as they are dear. In fact, they are a vital, essential part of our personal well-being.

Robert Fisher is admirably qualified to write on such a sensitive and needed theme. His scholastic and ecclesiastic qualifications are exceptional. His gifts of communication are evident on every page. Under the title *The Joy of Relationship*, he draws from the reservoir of a lifetime experience as counselor, pastor and administrator to illuminate his subject. In his writing one sees the heart of a teacher, pastor and friend, in which he does not hesitate to use the rich resources of his own life. The result is a trenchant, albeit gentle, work of scriptural emphasis and insight.

Without caviling with modern concepts that serve self more than God, or engaging in pop psychological solutions to dilemmas of the time, the author stakes out a course that centers in the eternal truths of God's Word. He also takes an incisive view of deterring notions and interpretations that disrupt spiritual joy and fulfillment; this makes the book a highly satisfying study of the very core of Christian life. I highly recommend it and wish for it a broad acceptance by the reading public.

—*Charles W. Conn*

ABOUT THIS BOOK

This book has been many years in the making. It comes out of a childhood of pain mixed with joy. It has evolved through over 40 years of marriage, ministry, family, and friendships during which each succeeding year brought a greater sense of fulfillment and happiness. At the center of all these experiences has been the intriguing dynamic of relationship.

Long ago I came to the conclusion that nothing in my life was more important than my relationship to God, to others, and to myself. Success or failure, satisfaction or frustration, I knew, flowed directly from the quality of my relationships. However, it was not until recent years that I began to understand the spiritual and theological significance of this matter. The more I studied what the Bible has to say about relationship, the greater the conviction grew in my heart that this subject was at the center of God's message to man.

Several years ago I began to do a lot of teaching and preaching on the Great Commandment, which embodies the Scriptural principles of relationship. Much of the material in this book is drawn from those messages. In all my study of this subject, I never found a book that addressed the practical application of these principles. That is what I hope this book does.

Let me say a word about the structure of this book. It contains numerous Scripture references. Since the Bible speaks so powerfully to this subject, it was important to undergird the applications presented with as much Scriptural truth as possible. There is quite a bit of repetition and reiteration of certain ideas and terms. This is done intentionally to underscore their importance. Finally, a number of personal illustrations are used. This was not planned in the original outline of the material, but as the book developed, these stories seemed to flow naturally into the content. Hopefully, they will shed some light that will be helpful.

At the back of the book is a set of study questions for each chapter. These were developed to assist the reader(s) in better understanding the material presented. They may be used to stimulate thinking and further study, and also as an aid in group discussion.

While this book was an intensely personal project, several persons are due special thanks. First, my wife Mary has taught me more than anyone about the practical aspect of relationships. She, our children, and our grandchildren have brought more joy into my life than I could ever have imagined was possible. I am proud of and grateful to my son Bob for his creativity in designing the cover and the page layout for the book.

At Pathway Press, Marcus Hand gave important insight through his editorial expertise, and Pat Bradbury was encouraging with her marketing skills. I also want to express my appreciation to Dr. Charles W. Conn for his graciousness in writing the Foreword. Finally, I owe two of my personal secretaries a particular note of thanks for their assistance: Pam Brewer early in the process and Kathy Isaacs in the final stages.

—Robert E. Fisher

INTRODUCTION

The Greatest Joy

* * *

*These things I have
spoken to you, that my
joy may remain in you,
and that your joy may be full.*

John 15:11 NKJV

CHAPTER 1

The Priority of Relationship

s I write the opening sentence of this book, I struggle immediately for the words to convey the absolute importance of this subject. Perhaps the best way is to put it simply and directly: "In life—and in death—*relationship is everything!*"

If you think that is an overstatement, consider Jesus' startling answer to the bottom-line question, "What is the greatest commandment?" He told his hearers that every commandment of the law and prophets is fulfilled through one transcending principle —a right relationship with God, with others and with oneself (Matt. 22:37-40).

The way we respond to this powerful truth affects every aspect of life. It determines our levels of happiness, our contentment, and our satisfaction. It controls the impact we make on others. It produces our self-image. More importantly, it serves as the basis for our final judgment before God.

All of life both now and forever is shaped by our understanding of and compliance with the greatest of all commandments: "'Love the Lord your God with all your heart . . . soul and . . . mind'; and, 'Love your neighbor as [much as you love] yourself'" (Luke 10:27).

An experience in my first pastorate produced some of my deepest hurts and, paradoxically, some of my greatest joys. Today, more than 30 years later, the reverberations of that experience still impact my life.

In that first church I succeeded a man who had died in office. His service with the congregation had been difficult, and his family was convinced that the pressures of the pastorate had contributed to his death. In their grief they questioned God and became bitter at some of the people whom the children perceived had opposed their father. This was particularly true of three grown sons who now assumed the leadership of the family.

As a young, inexperienced pastor I quickly found myself a target of their animosity. For some reason the family chose to remain in the church, and they understandably exercised considerable influence. While giving the impression of cooperation with the new pastor, they often found many ways to subtly oppose everything I tried to do. Opposition from one of the sons became intensely personal.

Stan Carver (not his real name) was outspoken in his disagreement with the direction I was leading the church. His indifference and disdainful facial expressions while I was preaching were tough to take. When my wife and I greeted the members of the congregation at the door following each Sunday morning service, we always experienced the same frustrating encounter with Stan: He would look straight ahead, walk on by, and totally ignore us. Most offensive was his refusal to shake my hand or acknowledge me as a person. He left by the side door of the church on one occasion, and I hurried to the parking lot to greet him and his family— only to have him roll up the car window in my face.

My first reaction to his behavior was fiery anger and deep resentment. After repeated encounters with his aloof contempt, my inclination was to punch him. Fortunately, the Lord gave me special grace, and I was able to restrain both my tongue and my fists. (I did, however, do my best not to look in his direction while I was preaching!)

One Sunday morning a great miracle happened. We had a moving service, and in the course of the message, I broke my rule and stole a quick glance in Stan's direction. To my absolute thrill I saw him brush aside a tear. Needless to say, it was with tremendous emotional and spiritual excitement following the service that I stood with my wife again greeting people at the door. I felt I was in a daze as other members of the congregation came by with smiles, hearty handshakes, and affirmative comments. I was waiting for that one former pastor's son who had been the bane of my existence.

My pulse began to race as I saw Stan approaching. Then he was in front of me. I smiled broadly and put out my hand with great expectation. To my utter shock and disappointment, he again walked past me and out the door without the slightest hint of acknowledgment. My heart sank and I was immediately overwhelmed with a combination of anger and despair.

Before I could regain my composure, however, the door burst open again, and that young man who had only moments before hurt me so deeply, now, without a word, flung his arms around me and with quiet sobs embraced me tightly. Finally he stepped back, wiped the tears from his eyes, and put his hands on my shoulders. He looked at me intently and said, "Pastor, you have won me! I promise you with God's help to be the best member you could ever have."

Stan kept that promise. He became one of the strongest leaders in the church. The unspeakable joy of being reconciled with that young man and that family exceeded even the wonderful experience of leading a united congregation in great growth over the next several years.

But this is not the end of the story! As happens so often, the positive implications of a loving relationship last a lifetime. Thirty years later the power of the restored relationship with that family in my first church reached across the thousands of miles separating us and miraculously influenced my life.

Recently, I had a serious accident involving my garden tractor which could well have resulted in extensive injuries or possibly even my death. But by undeniable divine intervention, I received not even the slightest scratch. Just a few hours after that traumatic experience, my sister, Joyce, called me long distance. "Bob," she asked anxiously, "are you all right?" I told her I was, but I wondered why she was asking. She went on to relate a remarkable story.

"This morning we had an unusual visit from Anthony Carver." He was another son of that former pastor. "We were surprised," she continued, "because we hadn't seen him in several years.

Almost immediately he asked about you. He told us he sensed that you were in danger and he had been awake most of the early morning hours praying for you. Because he couldn't get the matter off his mind and wasn't sure how to contact you, he decided to look us up."

I told Joyce the story of the tractor accident, and we cried together. She and her family had been a part of that first congregation and knew of my experience with the Carver family. She shared my amazement at the wondrous ways of God. We marveled at the providence of a gracious heavenly Father who can turn broken relationships into healing friendships that span earthly time and miles and literally reach into eternity.

God's Most Important Word to Man

Relationship is the practical theme of the Bible. From the first stories of man's calamitous alienation from God in the book of Genesis through the reconciling teachings of Jesus in the Gospels to the glorious eternal reunion depicted in Revelation, Scripture underscores the priority of relationship. Relationship to God, relationship to our fellow man, and relationship to ourself—like a golden thread these themes are woven through the pages of God's Word. Relationship is the key factor in the story of the first family, in the account of Jehovah and Israel, in the Ten Commandments and the Sermon on the Mount, and in the ultimate reality of heaven and hell.

While one could compile a lengthy list of Biblical illustrations underscoring the priority of relationship, nothing is more dramatic and specific than Jesus' own statement concerning the Great Commandment.

Jesus' critics were always asking Him difficult questions, but the one posed by the lawyer in Matthew 22:36 was probably the toughest of all. "Teacher," he asked, "which is the greatest commandment in the Law?" The answer Jesus gave forms the basis for this book.

Jesus' reply is extremely important for several reasons:

First, these are God's words, not the musings of a learned theologian or the hype of a pop psychologist.

Second, the answer deals with the most important of his words—the *greatest* commandment.

Third, His reply speaks in a practical way to the order and substance of the most vital issues of our lives: our relationships to God, to others, and to ourselves.

In answering the lawyer's question, Jesus referred to two Old Testament passages: "Love the Lord your God with all your heart and with all your soul and with all your strength" (Deuteronomy 6:5) and "love your neighbor as yourself" (Leviticus 19:18). Of all the commandments in the Old Testament, Jesus singled out these two. He put them together and called them the "greatest commandment." That should certainly catch our spiritual attention!

To emphasize even more strongly the importance of His reply, Jesus added this startling statement: "All the Law and the Prophets hang on these two commandments" (Matthew 22:40). Further, Jesus approved the pronouncement of the scribe that this greatest of all commandments "is more important than all burnt offerings and sacrifices" (Mark 12:33). In summary, the Son of God was saying that a right relationship with God, with others, and with oneself embodies the very essence of the Law and the Prophets and supersedes in importance any ritual of worship.

Since right relationships top God's list of important things, it stands to reason that Christians should make them their prime objective. Unfortunately, that is often not the case. The devil is adept at distracting us. He does his best to scramble our priorities and get us off on spiritual rabbit trails that lead to disappointment and disillusionment. Keeping relational priorities in order is the key to personal happiness and spiritual success.

Violate This Order and You're in Trouble

God is the God of order. The intricate workings of the universe testify eloquently to this fact. When God's order is disrupted or violated, whether in the mighty cosmos or in everyday human behavior, momentous problems always ensue.

In His enunciating the greatest commandment, Jesus noted a specific order in relationships. He said we are to love God first, then others, and finally ourself. Love implies a proper, balanced relationship in all three areas. First things must be put first. It has been said that "the main thing is to keep the main thing the main thing."

Love God first and best. That may sound simple, but it is not. When we experience difficulties with others or we battle low self-esteem, the temptation is to deal with the problem at the horizontal level rather than immediately checking the vertical relationship. We tend to believe that human problems have human solutions. So when trouble arises in our marriage or with our children, we search the newspaper for what Ann Landers or Dear Abby may have to say, or we rush to the bookstore to buy the appropriate new book. When we are devastated by feelings of failure and inferiority, we rack our brains for an answer and feel we should somehow be able to pull ourselves up by our own bootstraps.

The answer to these dilemmas, according to God's order in the great commandment, is not the outward look (to others) or the inward look (to self), but the upward look (to God). When things go wrong on the horizontal level, God's admonition is for us to move arbitrarily to the vertical level. "But seek first his kingdom and his righteousness, and all these things will be given to you as well" (Matthew 6:33).

It is not easy to shift from the horizontal to the vertical—to change our focus even momentarily from the human to the divine. This requires a conscious act of the will: "I will stop thinking about my human problems and limitations and will focus my thinking instead on God's love and His resources." This kind of effort to obey God's Word brings an immediate sense of relief and strength. This is not mind over matter. It is an act of simple faith that says, "God is bigger than any of my problems, and my relationship with Him is the most important thing in my life."

Everything, from the act of cosmic creation (Genesis 1:1; John 1:1) to the art of daily living, begins with God. The Scriptural order always and eternally is: God, others, self. The secular humanists of our day reverse this order and tell us to begin with self. Their philosophy (which is in reality a theology) is that as we become self-actualized and discover our own inner powers, we are better able to relate to others. In that improved relationship with others, we may perhaps understand the essence of "god."

Buying into that philosophy/theology is at the heart of the frightening problems plaguing modern society. The increase in crime, the abuse of drugs, preoccupation with sex and violence, the disintegration of the family—these deadly scourges of our contemporary world can be traced directly to the practice of the humanistic credo which holds that man is capable of self-fulfillment and of setting his own ethical and moral standards. William Glasser states that the 20th century has seen an unprecedented cultural shift from a *goal*-oriented society to a *role*-oriented society. No longer is man concerned primarily with achieving certain goals for himself, his family, and his country. His driving passion now is his own role—his rights, his needs, his fulfillment.

This flagrant violation of God's commandment, this reversal of God's order, has created problems of such horrific proportions that they threaten the very future of our civilized world. We have sown to the wind, and we are now beginning to reap the whirlwind.

While the worldwide scope of these problems deeply concerns us, the personalized aspect of this order-reversal gives us the greatest pain. We witness daily the devastating effect of this self-focus in the lives of those closest to us and in our own personal life. This deadly spiritual disease infects and, in many cases, destroys marriages, families, and friendships. It has, in turn, robbed us of our peace, our hope, and our self-esteem. God did not intend it to be this way.

Practice This Order and Reap the Benefits

The simple Scriptural order of God, others, and self produces remarkably positive results when we put it into practice. I have seen lives transformed, marriages restored, self-confidence gained, and true happiness achieved when people changed their behavior to meet God's standard.

God taught me this lesson of Scriptural order in a dramatic

way. Serving as a pastor some years ago, I was riding a wave of spiritual and numerical success in my church. Everything seemed to be going right. It appeared that the sky was the limit. We were experiencing record-breaking crowds, vibrant worship services, tremendous spiritual results, and gratifying personal accolades. I was overwhelmed. I had never been happier or had a greater sense of fulfillment.

On a particular Sunday that wave reached a crest. I went to sleep that Sunday night basking in a feeling of satisfaction I had never experienced before. When I awoke on Monday morning, the euphoria continued. The grass was greener, the sky was bluer, and the birds sang more sweetly than I could ever remember.

Then the telephone rang. It was the church treasurer—one of my closest friends and most ardent supporters. I was glad to hear his voice and anticipated positive remarks. Instead of affirming words, I received the most ravaging rebuke of my life. For several minutes this church leader excoriated me with words articulated in such a manner that I still feel them in my heart today. He would not let me speak, and when he finished, he hung up. I tried to call back, but his line was busy.

About the time he hung up, my wife walked into the room. She sensed something was wrong. "Who was that?" she asked. "What's going on?" I was too drained spiritually, psychologically, and physically to talk about it. I had to be by myself. In a moment everything had changed. My overwhelming joy had been replaced by a pain too deep to describe.

I got into my car and headed for the church office a few miles away. I was so overcome I could hardly drive. A flood of tears made it difficult to see. In the midst of that great personal trauma,

I sensed the presence of the Lord with me in the car. In my spirit, we began an unusual conversation.

"Why are you so upset?"

"Lord, You know why. It's Frank."

"Frank? What has Frank got to do with this?"

"Lord, You know. He's the church treasurer. He's one of the most influential persons in the church."

"Yes, I know about Frank, but what about your relationship with Me?"

"Lord, You know I love You. But Frank . . ."

"Forget Frank for a minute. Let Me ask you another question. Has anything changed between you and Me in the past 15 minutes?"

"No, Lord."

"Then where is your joy? Am I not the same God I was 15 minutes ago?"

"Yes, Lord."

"All right then. If I haven't changed and your relationship with Me hasn't changed, I want you to have the same sense of joy you had before Frank called."

"But, Lord . . ."

"Here's what I want you to do. I want you to sing a happy song. Furthermore, I want you to whistle."

"But, Lord . . ."

"Do it!"

Singing, let alone whistling, was the farthest thing from my mind at that moment. But I knew God had spoken to me. I struggled to get the first few words out of my mouth. Then the song began to flow more freely. I stopped crying.

What about the whistling? At first, it felt like I had a mouthful of crackers. But I persisted. I whistled. I sang. I praised the Lord. I started to cry again, but this time it was with tears of thankfulness and worship. My dark mood was broken. My spirit soared.

By the time I got to my office, my joy had returned in bountiful measure. Instead of falling on the floor and burying my face in the carpet, I stood on my tiptoes praising and worshiping the God who was so real in my life. Then the telephone rang. It was Frank. He begged my forgiveness. He apologized profusely. He explained that he had had an argument with his father and didn't know why he had taken out his frustrations on me. We prayed together, and the matter was settled never to be mentioned again.

God had burned a truth into my heart that is just as relevant today as it was on that eventful day. Now every time I am shaken by a harsh criticism or inundated by feelings of self-doubt, I check my relationship with the Lord. If everything is OK there, I feel my strength and confidence returning. It's amazing how it works every time.

God's relationship order produces a sequence of characteristics vital to successful living:

• A proper relationship with God has to do with *being*. Who we really are will determine how we behave. We cannot bear good fruit without being grafted into the True Vine.

• A proper relationship with others has to do with *doing*. Being good always results in doing good. We cannot love God without loving our brother, our spouse, our children, even our enemies (1 John 4:20, 21).

• A proper relationship with oneself has to do with *feeling*. A sense of confidence and happiness comes directly from knowing that things are right with God and with others.*

These concepts will be explored in depth in succeeding chapters. Let us look next at one of the most powerful by-products of proper relationships—the fruit of joy.

*This order of relationship is summarized in a chart on page 177.

CHAPTER 2

The Power of Joy

J oy is a difficult word to define. It is deeper than pleasure. It is more distinct than happiness. C.S. Lewis in his book, *Surprised by Joy*, describes a joyful experience of his childhood as "a delight that tingled down the spine and troubled the belly and at moments went near to stopping the breath" (p. 36). Joy is something wonderfully positive and pure. It lifts the spirit and heals the soul. In simple terms it can perhaps best be defined as "a deep sense of satisfaction and contentment."

Joy is a much sought after commodity—one which unfortunately is sadly lacking in many lives, even in the lives of those who are Christians. The presence or absence of joy in one's life is determined primarily by the quality of one's relationships. Relationships (with God, others, and self) bring us our highest highs and our lowest lows. The psalms of David vividly illustrate this point.

God intended for relationships to be joyful. His ideal is that, with a proper perspective, all of them can produce a sense of satisfaction and contentment. Regardless of the circumstances or the persons involved, every relationship (even those with enemies) can be handled in a way that minimizes pain and maximizes satisfaction. We don't have to accept them as they are handed to us. God can give us the wisdom and strength to shape and improve our relationships. As a result, a melody of joy will begin to ring in our heart. We will be able to sing with conviction the little chorus I learned when I first became a Christian:

On Sunday I am happy, on Monday full of joy,
On Tuesday I have peace within that nothing can destroy;
On Wednesday and on Thursday I'm walking in the light,
On Friday is a heav'n below, and Saturday's always bright.

The Scriptural approach is not a formula to rid us of all problems. What I propose in this chapter (and in this book) will not put us above the battle, floating on a spiritual cloud somewhere in space. God's truth when practiced will give us the ability to cope in the toughest of circumstances, however. We can cope when it seems our faith is gone and God is nowhere to be found, when we are psychologically battered and spiritually bruised in family relationships, and when feelings of failure overwhelm us like a flood. I am not talking about perpetual happiness. But I am stating unequivocally that the child of God can be sustained every day of his life by a deep sense of satisfaction and contentment—a genuine joy that is truly unspeakable and full of glory.

Attaining this lofty spiritual goal is not an easy task. It requires a solid Scriptural knowledge coupled with a tenacious personal discipline. But don't worry, God will provide both if we will open ourselves to the leadership of His Holy Spirit.

The Upward Source of Joy

We return to the simple God-others-self pattern established by Jesus. The primary source of joy is the relationship one has with God. Over and over the Bible characterizes our relationship with God as one of joy and satisfaction. "With joy you will draw water from the wells of salvation" (Isaiah 12:3).

Too often we approach God as if He were an enemy or, at best, an angry judge. He has assured us He is a friend (John 15:9). He has promised to give us relief when we go to Him loaded down with the cares of life (Matthew 11:28). He says this relationship is easy, not difficult (v. 30). When the people of Israel became afraid that they couldn't measure up to the Word of God, Nehemiah counseled them to remember that "the joy of the Lord is your strength" (Nehemiah 8:10).

A series of problems put a friend of mine in a state of deep depression at one point in his life. He had no appetite. He couldn't sleep, and he couldn't pray. Finally, in the middle of a sleepless night he decided he was going to have it out with the Lord. He got up and drove to the church he was attending. He had a key, so he let himself in and started walking around the darkened sanctuary. For what seemed like hours, nothing happened. The creaks in the empty building and the flashing of a nearby traffic light distracted him, and he became even more frustrated.

Then an idea struck him. He went to one of the rooms designated for prayer. He pulled two folding chairs aside and placed them facing each other. He sat in one chair and told the Lord he believed He was sitting in the other. He didn't pray as he had been doing for several weeks—pleading, crying, angry, sullenly quiet. He started talking to the Lord as he would to his closest friend, and the Lord responded in kind. He knew God was there. He envisioned the Lord's compassionate gaze. He saw Him smiling and reaching out to touch him. He said he fell at Jesus' feet and began to rejoice. He was miraculously healed and delivered from his psychological and spiritual depression. If he had only known, God was there all the time.

> Though the fig tree does not bud and there are no grapes on the vines, though the olive crop fails and the fields produce no food, though there are no sheep in the pen and no cattle in the stalls, yet I will rejoice in the Lord, I will be joyful in God my Savior (Habbakuk 3:17, 18).

Just before Jesus went to the cross, He spent a lot of time teaching, fellowshipping with, and praying for His disciples. He was preparing them for the tough times ahead. Five chapters (13-17) in the book of John are devoted to the historical record of Jesus' message to His followers. Read those chapters again, taking Jesus' words personally as you prepare for what lies ahead in your life.

Jesus talked about joy a number of times in this discourse. He told the questioning disciples, "I tell you the truth, you will weep and mourn while the world rejoices. You will grieve, but your grief will turn to joy" (John 16:20).

He emphasized the importance of understanding the relationship He would have with them: "I have told you this so that my joy may be in you and that your joy may be complete" (John 15:11).

Anticipating the coming of Jesus the Messiah, David wrote, "You have made known to me the path of life; you will fill me with joy in your presence, with eternal pleasures at your right hand" (Psalm 16:11).

Nothing in life is more basic than our relationship with God. It stands above all other relationships—those with husband, wife, children, closest friends. In the intensely personal world where self-image is shaped, evaluations must be made first from God's perspective. All input from others and self must be secondary. God is the primary source of everything in life including truth, faith, hope, love, and joy.

The next time you find yourself without joy and all the emotional wells seem dry, take God at His Word and draw from His boundless supply. "Then my soul will rejoice in the Lord and delight in his salvation" (Psalm 35:9).

The Outward Source of Joy

While most of us have had some truly aesthetic experiences and have derived a sense of joy from an object of art or the beauty of nature, our deepest joys in the earthly realm usually come from relationships with other people. The reverse is true as well, however, because other people also bring us our deepest hurts.

It is important to note that we are not at the mercy of others with regard to those joys and hurts. As free moral agents we have the power to control our response to the behavior of others. We cannot control them—even God doesn't do that—but we can and should control our response to them. We have the privilege of accentuating the positive and eliminating the negative in our relationships with others.

Paul exercised that right in his relationship with the church at Thessalonica. In establishing this church, he suffered life-threatening persecution. As the church developed, false teachers who opposed Paul gained prominence. However, when he wrote back to the church he chose not to focus on past or present difficulties, but rather to express his deep love for the people. "For what is our hope, our joy, or the crown in which we will glory in the presence of our Lord Jesus when he comes?" Paul asked. "Is it not you? Indeed you are our glory and joy" (1 Thessalonians 2:19, 20).

In his letter to the church at Philippi, Paul told the people: "I thank my God every time I remember you" (1:3). He called them his "joy and crown" (4:1). Had Paul forgotten the Philippian jail, the severe beatings, the attempts on his life? No, he had not forgotten; he simply chose to think on the true, noble, and just things—on the good reports (4:8). He recognized that he had enemies, and he did not hesitate to confront negative issues; but he did not make those things the focus on his life or his letter. Paul himself was in prison, facing death when he wrote the Philippian epistle. Although he was in physical chains, the joy of his relationship with the Philippians transcended earthly circumstance and set his spirit free.

Paul's approach to his relationship with others is as relevant today as it was in his day because it is Scriptural. It is God's pattern. Notice three basic elements that form a pattern: *responsibility, control,* and *prayer.*

If we expect to have a joyful relationship with others we must do our best to fulfill our responsibilities to the relationship. In his letter to the church at Thessalonica, Paul rehearsed the record of his behavior: "You are witnesses, and God also, how devoutly and justly and blamelessly we behaved ourselves among you who believe" (1 Thesssalonians 2:10, *NKJV*). He did this not to brag on himself, but to point out the importance of individual responsibility.

Much is said today about *rights* but little about *responsibilities.* Like many other two-edged swords, we cannot expect our rights to be protected without first fulfilling our responsibilities. When things go wrong in a relationship, the human tendency is to place blame on the other person. This response has many negative implications, but the worst of which is that it takes the focus off the blamer's responsibilities in the matter. In judgment God will not ask us about the behavior of others. The singular question will be "What did *you* do?" "So then each of us shall give account of *himself* to God" (Romans 14:12, *NKJV*).

The fulfillment of individual responsibility is foundational to the success of any relationship. It is also the seed from which joy will spring. It is not a matter of being perfect in the fulfillment of responsibilities; it is that this priority must be set. My primary obligation in a relationship is to do my part to the best of my ability, regardless of the behavior of the other person. I must strive to bear good fruit and trust it to have a salutary effect upon the relationship.

Another important element in producing joy in a relationship is *control.* I cannot control the behavior of other people (although I may waste a lot of time trying), but I can control my own behavior. Just as importantly, I can control my response to their behavior.

Paul chose to give people the benefit of the doubt. He complimented them. He expressed his gratitude for their support. But most of all he lavished his love on them. Over and over he called them his "beloved." They were obviously not perfect people, but Paul made a conscious decision to concentrate on their good points—not just in his letter, but also in his thinking. That is key. It is an easy thing to write nice things on a birthday or anniversary card, but the question is "Do I really believe those things and demonstrate them in my every day behavior?"

Paul made this practice part of his theology. "Finally, brothers, whatever is true, whatever is noble, whatever is right, whatever is pure, whatever is lovely, whatever is admirable—if anything is excellent or praiseworthy—think about such things" (Philippians 4:8).

There can be little joy in a relationship where thinking is dominated by negatives and where criticism is consistently verbalized. Whether we will acknowledge it or not, we can control what goes on in our head and what comes out of our mouth. We have a choice: we can obey the Word of God, think on good things, and reap a harvest of happiness and joy; or we can disobey His commands, think on bad things, and reap a harvest of misery and woe. If this sounds too simplistic or idealistic, check with the apostle Paul.

A third element in joyful relationships is *prayer*. Again, Paul demonstrated this in his writings. "I thank my God upon every remembrance of you, always in every prayer of mine making request for you all with joy" (Philippians 1:3, 4, *NKJV*). It is not difficult to pray for friends, although too often we neglect that privilege and pray only when there are difficulties. The really tough part that seems so unreasonable is to pray for our enemies. Jesus said, "But I tell you: Love your enemies and pray for those who persecute you" (Matthews 5:44).

In Jesus' revolutionary teaching concerning the handling of enemies, He not only told us to pray for them, but to counter their opposition with joy. When we are persecuted, we are to "rejoice and be exceedingly glad" (Matthew 5:12, *NKJV*). The apostles practiced Jesus' teachings. "So they departed from the presence of the council, rejoicing that they were counted worthy to suffer shame for His name" (Acts 5:41, *NKJV*). James says, "My brethren, count it all joy when you fall into various trials" (James 1:2, *NKJV*). Prayer, coupled with clear thinking, produces a perspective that neutralizes the most negative situation and brings joy instead of depression.

So much of how we feel about life depends on our relationship with others. Following God's plan guarantees that joy will predominate those relationships.

The Inward Source of Joy

Relationship with God and with others determines how one feels about himself. None of us operates in a vacuum. The philosopher John Donne declared, "No man is an island." Despite what New Agers or secular humanists may say, man cannot begin with himself or look solely to himself for fulfillment and satisfaction. Someone has said, "The smallest package I have ever seen is a man wrapped up in himself." We need only to go to a mental institution to see the ultimate tragic results of a person totally focused on self. Regardless of one's mental state, egocentrism is a disease that plagues us all.

While there is this problem with self, the Bible makes it clear that God wants us to feel good about ourself. "For God did not give us a spirit of timidity, but a spirit of power, of love and of self discipline" (2 Timothy 1:7). God does not want his children to suffer from a poor self-image or from feelings of inferiority. "Finally, be strong in the Lord and in his mighty power" (Ephesians 6:10).

One of the most powerful weapons the devil uses against

believers is the "big putdown." He is called in Scripture "the accuser" (Revelation 12:10), and he works overtime at this job. It is difficult to experience much joy in life when one is struggling with low self-esteem. Even when something good happens, it is immediately negated by the notion that it is not deserved. When the angel of the Lord spoke to Gideon and called him a "mighty man of valor" who was to save Israel, Gideon's reply was, "But Lord, how can I save Israel? My clan is the weakest in Manasseh, and I am the least in my family" (Judges 6:15). How like Gideon we are.

Instead of feeling badly about ourself, God wants us to derive joy from the strong self-image He gives us in our relationship with Him. The apostle Paul got a lot of joy out of remembering his relationships with fellow believers, but it is also evident that he rejoiced in his own accomplishments. He rejoiced in even his adversities. "That is why, for Christ's sake, I delight in weaknesses, in insults, in hardships, in persecutions, in difficulties. For when I am weak, then I am strong" (2 Corinthians 12:10).

Paul used the word "I" frequently, yet he wasn't bragging. He recounted on numerous occasions his encounter with the Lord on the Damascus road, and each time he seemed to get great satisfaction out of telling it again. He knew how to squeeze a lot of happiness out of remembering his exploits in the Lord. He told the Philippians, "Rejoice in the Lord always. I will say it again:, Rejoice" (4:4). He certainly practiced what he preached to them. Paul Rees, in his book, *The Adequate Man*, says the writing of Paul to the church at Philippi "gives to any sensitive reader a feeling of the sheer joy there is in a life which Christ has redeemed and within which He resides through His Spirit" (p. 12).

For years my wife has been recording photographically the

important events of our family. She not only takes the pictures, but she organizes them in albums. A lot of people do that, but Mary goes a step further. She adds a narrative. She tells the story of the pictures. One of these albums traces the history of the homes in which we have lived during the course of our marriage —from the first motel room in which we lived after our honeymoon to our present home. In essence, this historical record is the story of our life together. Every time I look through those pictures and read that story, I cry. I've probably repeated that ritual 50 times, and each time I vow I won't cry again. But I always do. I can't help it. Those photographs remind me of how good God has been to me and my family. They remind me that God keeps his promises. In my remembrance, I am overwhelmed with joy; my cup runs over.

The inward source of joy can be very satisfying. You should not rob yourself of its pleasures. Inexplicable happiness comes from knowing that God has laid his hand on you personally—that you are a chosen vessel. He will continue to bless you in the future as He has in the past.

God wants to send a liberating flow of joy into your life through your relationships. He will help you discover how to take advantage of all the sources—upward, outward, and inward.

PART 1

Loving God

* * *

*Love the Lord your God
with all your heart and
with all your soul and
with all your strength.*

—Deuteronomy 6:5

CHAPTER 3

Centering Your Affection

W hat is the top priority in the life of a Christian? There can be no doubt about the answer to this question. Jehovah God made it very clear in the Old Testament, and his son Jesus repeated it in the New. It is to "love the Lord your God." First! Foremost! Above everything else! That sounds simple enough. No big deal. Anyone can do that.

The truth of the matter is, it is a big deal—the biggest deal of all. Nothing is more important. Everything in life hinges on our obeying this commandment—the first of God's most important words to man. This is where we start.

Loving God First

To really love God means to make Him the center of your life. The Scripture puts it this way: "Set your affection on things above, not on things on the earth" (Colossians 3:2, *KJV*). This means to fix

43

your mind and heart on heavenly, spiritual things. The idea is to make a conscious effort to focus first on God—at the beginning of every day, in the consideration of every major decision, and at the outset of every life encounter. In a world filled with so many distractions, this is not an easy thing to do.

Solomon gave wise counsel in this regard: "Let your eyes look straight ahead, fix your gaze directly before you. Make level paths for your feet and take only ways that are firm. Do not swerve to the right or the left; keep your foot from evil" (Proverbs 4:25-27).

The devil is good at creating distractions. He will do whatever he can to divert your attention from the good to the bad, from the positive to the negative, and from the spiritual to the worldly. He does this primarily through outside influences—what you see and what you hear. But he will also work on your mind and impact your emotions.

In John Bunyan's classic tale, *The Pilgrim's Progress*, the main character, Christian (representing every believer), is constantly tempted to turn aside in his journey from the City of Destruction to the City of Zion. If the temptation is not discouragement from falling into the Slough of Despond, then it is an outright battle with the monster Apollyon. In one episode he encounters Mr. Worldly Wiseman who tries to convince Christian to turn aside from his commitment and find a less difficult and dangerous way to reach his spiritual goal.

> *Worldly Wiseman:* But why wilt thou seek for ease this way, seeing so many dangers attend it, especially since, hadst thou but patience to hear me, I could direct thee to the obtaining of what thou desirest, without the dangers that thou in this way wilt run thyself into; yea, and the remedy

is at hand. Besides, I will add, that instead of these dangers thou shall meet with much safety, friendship and content (p. 21).

Poor Christian took the advice of Mr. Worldly Wiseman, left his journey on the straight path, and, for a time, lost his heavenly vision. He soon discovered the fallacy of worldly wisdom in contrast to the powerful, practical truth of God's law.

Giving priority to our relationship with God is the best road to happiness and success. It is the only road to the eternal City of Zion.

Remember that no other relationship will be right until you seek first the face of God. The next time you encounter a difficulty in relationship on the horizontal level (with a spouse, son, daughter, friend, or enemy), forget that problem for a moment and concentrate on the vertical relationship—the one with your heavenly Father. It is not a matter of simply thinking about God, but rather of checking up on the relationship to see if there are any obstacles—any instances of disobedience, any unconfessed sins.

The wonderful part about this kind of spiritual check is that it doesn't require weeks, days, or even hours to fix a strained or broken relationship with God. His understanding is guaranteed. His forgiveness is instantaneous. If you will do this spiritual exercise intentionally and deliberately, you will experience an immediate, miraculous change in your attitude and your feelings. Loving God first will give you a whole different perspective on how you feel about others and how you feel about yourself.

I heard of a mother who felt conviction because of hurtful things she frequently said to her nine-year-old son when he misbehaved. She knew her behavior was detrimental to her relation-ship with her son and to his self-image, but she also understood that she was sinning against God in her anger toward her son. She had tried many times to control her rage. She had made promises to herself and to her son. Nothing seemed to help. One afternoon she felt she had finally found the key. After a considerable time of prayer, she truly confessed and repented. For the first time in many months, she knew things were right between her and her Lord.

As she basked in the warmth of God's presence, the front door opened and slammed shut, shaking the whole house. Billy was home from school. She felt a flood of anger sweep over her. *How many times have I told him not to slam that door!* she thought.

Billy came into the den where she was and without a word, threw his lunch pail on the floor. Before she could respond to this seeming defiance, he ran down the hallway to his room and delib-erately slammed that door.

I'm going to get that kid, she said to herself. *He knows better than that!*

She started towards his room, her temper raging. As she was about to open the door to his bedroom the Spirit of God arrested her. She remembered her confession and God's forgiveness. She paused in the hallway and suddenly felt her anger receding and spiritual strength flowing into her.

After a few minutes, she quietly opened the bedroom door. Billy was lying across his bed, face down, sobbing softly. She sat down beside him and gently rubbed his back. Finally he looked up and wiped the tears from his cheeks.

"What's the matter, son?" she asked.

"Mom, this has been the worst day of my life. I failed my math test, and my best friend told me he didn't like me anymore."

On that day a mother learned a lesson that forever changed her relationship with her son. She found that loving God first was the secret to a joyful relationship with others.

A Matter of the Heart

God outlines an order in relationships with others, but He also gives an order to the way a Christian loves God. In all the parallel passages about loving God, note that we are to love God first with all our *heart.*

The heart, as used in these scriptures, generally refers to the seat of the affections, the feeling parts of consciousness. It has to do with strong emotion and intense devotion. The implication is that we are to love God from our innermost being. David demonstrated the intensity of this kind of love when he poured out his heart in Psalm 103: "Bless the Lord, O my soul: and all that is within me, bless his holy name" (v. 1, *KJV*).

It is significant that God says we are to love him first with the feeling aspect of our nature. So it is not first a matter of the head, but a matter of the heart. Loving God is not first intellectual, but emotional. It is not an external rite of worship, but a cry of adoration from the deep recesses of the soul. This is a radical kind of love that seems at times to defy reason and logic. Listen to the apostle Paul as he expresses his strong feelings about his relationship with the Lord:

> But what things were gain to me, those I counted loss for
> Christ. Yea doubtless, and I count all things but loss for the

excellency of the knowledge of Christ Jesus my Lord: for whom I have suffered the loss of all things, and do count them but dung, that I may win Christ . . . That I may know him, and the power of his resurrection, and the fellowship of his sufferings, being made conformable unto his death" (Philippians 3:7, 8, 10, *KJV*).

Paul had come to realize that "things" were standing in the way of his full devotion to Christ. These were not necessarily bad things, but they took priority in his heart over his relationship with God. So Paul moved aside these distractions; he counted them as "rubbish" (v. 8, *NIV*) when compared to his love for Christ.

The heart of the Protestant Reformation was the so-called "Copernican revolution" which replaced works and the church as focal points of the Christian universe with Christ and His grace. The church today, along with the individual believer, must get back to that first love where an intensity of commitment to God naturally flows from loving the Lord with all one's heart.

The message to the church at Ephesus in Revelation 2 makes this very point. The Lord commended the Ephesian church for their hard work, patience, perseverance, and purity of doctrine. However, those Christians were rebuked for leaving their foundational relationship with Christ. They were admonished to repent and to do again their first works.

Matthew Henry talks about the meaning of "first love" and "first works:" "The first affections of men towards Christ, and holiness, and heaven, are usually lively and warm. God remembered the love of Israel's espousals, when she would follow him withersoever he went. These lively affections will abate and cool if great care be not taken . . . Christ is grieved and displeased with his people when he sees them grow remiss and cold towards Him and He will one way or other make them sensible that He does not take it well from them" (p. 2465).

It is a serious matter when a Christian loses his "first love." The people of the Ephesian church were warned that if they did not repent and straighten out their relationship with the Lord, their "lampstand" would be removed. They would no longer be a church representing the gospel of Christ. They had gotten their priorities out of order. Even though they were working hard and their declaration of faith was sound, still they were in danger of losing God's presence and anointing. They were devoted to His work, but they were not devoted to Him.

If you think God's judgment in this matter sounds too harsh, think of Jesus' statement concerning those who claimed they had done many wonderful works in his name. Because they had failed to do the will of the Father, despite their work, He said to them in judgment: "I never knew you: depart from me" (Matthew 7:23, *KJV*).

If our relationship with God is not based first of all on a heartfelt love, it will soon deteriorate into a lifeless ritual which is spiritually dangerous to us and sorely displeasing to God. It takes a constant, vigilant effort on our part to keep that love for God fervent, intense, and fresh.

Keep in mind that this first-step relationship with God—loving him with all your heart—is foundational to every other level of relationship. It is also the source of our greatest and most enduring joy. Whatever the difficulty you may be facing at this moment, whatever the pressure or the trauma, it will fade into insignificance as you love the Lord with all your heart. Why not do that right now? Bless Him! Praise Him! Worship Him! Adore Him! Magnify His holy name!

> Turn your eyes upon Jesus,
> Look full in His wonderful face,
> And the things of earth will grow strangely dim
> In the light of His glory and grace. —*Helen H. Lemmell*

The Focus of Your Emotion

One of the watershed experiences of my life happened a few years ago when I was attending a conference in London. Because of a telephone call, I had missed the shuttle bus to the conference center one night, so I had to take the subway. Here I was, away from home and family, in another country and an unfamiliar city, riding on a train with 20 or 30 other people, none of whom I knew. All of a sudden, without any warning, I was totally overwhelmed by the presence of God in a way that had never happened to me before. It affected me physically, as well as emotionally and spiritually. I felt dizzy and shaky, but I knew immediately it was not a physical problem. I started to cry and couldn't control my tears. The most predominant feeling, however, was a sense of joy and exultation on a level I had not experienced before. In my spirit I felt God impressing me to go back to my hotel room. I got off the train at the next stop and boarded another one going the opposite direction. I could hardly contain my spiritual excitement.

When I got to the hotel, I literally ran to my room. For some time I lay across the bed, rejoicing in the presence of the Lord. My emotions ran the gamut. I cried for joy. I sobbed with a heavy burden. I sang. I prayed. I praised. Through it all, I sensed the voice of God speaking to me about his will and purpose for my life. The impact of that experience remains with me today. In fact, just a few days ago I was reminded again of a promise that came to me during that time with the Lord.

I am not an emotional person by nature. As a young man, I had a difficult time receiving the infilling of the Holy Spirit because I was concerned about getting "in the flesh." I resisted spiritual manifestations. But that experience in London taught me a lesson about my relationship with God. I am convinced that anytime a human being comes in contact with the Spirit of God, there will be an emotional response. The Bible is full of examples to support this fact. Religious history verifies that through the centuries man's encounter with God has usually begun at the heart/emotion/feeling level.

Loving God with all our heart is foundational to all other aspects of our relationship with God. This is His plan, His order, not ours. It is interesting that God uses our feelings and emotions as the beginning point of our relationship with him. This part of our human nature is the one most prone to excesses and to spiritual highs and lows. It is generally the most unstable aspect of our personality.

The religious enthusiasm of people during times of revival and spiritual renewal often poses problems for leaders. But this is the door of entry God has chosen. If this emotional and devotional dynamic is suppressed or missing in our walk with God, our relationship will never have the fullness and completeness God intends. This emotional response to God has been characterized as the initial flame that ignites a fire, then subsides, like charcoal, to make the coals useful.

In the next chapter we will see that loving God with all our heart is only the first step. We must go from there to an ever strengthening and maturing relationship with the Lord. Jonathan Edwards, early American revivalist, wrote about the balance between religious enthusiasm and the outflow of good works. Some of Edwards' writings on the subject, from his *Thoughts on the Revival in New England* (1742) and *A Treatise Concerning Religious Affections* (1746), are summarized by Richard Lovelace:

> Experiences of renewal which are genuinely from the Holy Spirit are God-centered in character, based on worship, an appreciation of God's worth and grandeur divorced from self-interest. Such experiences create humility in the convert rather than pride and issue in the creation of a new spirit of meekness, gentleness, forgiveness and mercy. They leave the believer hungering and thirsting after righteousness instead of satiated with self-congratulation (p. 42).

It is a wonderful thing to feel a spiritual connection with Almighty God. However, it must produce more in us than shallow emotionalism or self-righteous pride. One of the surest ways to keep a Scriptural balance in this basic area of our relationship with God is through our practice of the spiritual disciplines and personal devotions.

The Object of Your Devotion

Devotion is a step beyond emotion in loving God with all our heart. It tends to be more active than passive in our approach to God. It requires initiative on our part, rather than simple response. Devotion can be defined as an "ardent dedication or loyalty to someone or something."

Devotion to God is generally practiced through the exercise of the spiritual disciplines of prayer, fasting, study, and meditation. Our love for God is demonstrated by the initiative we take in endeavoring to draw close to God and to know him better.

One of the most obvious ways to strengthen our relationship with the Lord is through the discipline of prayer. We must always keep in mind that the primary object of prayer is to focus on the glory and the goodness of God. When the disciples asked Jesus to teach them to pray, he gave them what is often referred to as the "Lord's Prayer" (Matthew 6:9-13). This model prayer, which would more correctly be called the "disciples' prayer," begins and ends with the emphasis on God. These are the opening words: "Our Father in heaven, hallowed be your name. Your kingdom come. Your will be done on earth as it is in heaven." The closing words are "For Yours is the kingdom and the power and the glory forever. Amen" (*NKJV*). When we pray, we must remember that our purpose is not to focus on ourselves and our needs, but upon the Father and our responsibility to Him.

As incongruous as it may seem, it is possible for prayer to become self-serving and even an affront to God. Jesus warned his disciples about this: "And when you pray, do not be like the hypocrites, for they love to pray standing in the synagogues and on the street corners to be seen by men. I tell you the truth, they have received their reward in full" (Matthew 6:5).

One of the most arresting chapters in the entire Bible is Isaiah 58. In it God gives a scathing rebuke to Israel for her attitude toward God and His house. The Israelites were doing all the right things, but for the wrong reasons. They were praying, fasting, paying their tithes, and attending church. But God rejected them and their works because of their bad attitude and contemptuous behavior. While God severely rebukes Israel, he also gives them some fantastic promises if they will repent. If you haven't read Isaiah 58 recently, I suggest you do so as soon as possible. It has a strong message for Christians and for the church today.

Now we are ready to take the second step in our relationship with God—from loving God with all our *heart* to loving God with all our *soul*. We follow His Word to fulfill His will.

CHAPTER 4

Giving Your Life

His life had been one of deceit and deception. He was always making deals with twists to them that were calculated to turn in his favor. He had been separated from his family early on because of his part in a conspiracy to defraud his brother. Wherever he went, he was looking over his shoulder, expecting some of his past to catch up with him. It was not a very pleasant way to live.

Now he was in a real panic. The thing he had feared for so many years was about to come upon him. Judgment day had arrived. His daughter had been raped. His older sons had taken things into their own hands. With great vengeance they had murdered and plundered. His enemies were mounting armies against him. He and his entire family were about to be destroyed. The weighty accumulation of all his past deeds was about to come down upon his head.

Jacob did what most of us would do in a situation like this; he cried out to God. He had done that many times before, but this time it was different. Jacob had reached a watershed moment in his life. This time when God spoke, Jacob fully obeyed, and his life was never the same. After he had purified his household, he began a journey back to Bethel, where he had first met God. He was delivered from the hand of his enemies, and when he arrived at Bethel, he built a new altar there. He made a fresh and lasting commitment to Jehovah God. He was no longer Jacob, the supplanter and deceiver. Now he was Israel, the prince of God.

This dramatic spiritual moment in the life of Jacob demonstrates what Jesus meant when he said we were to love God with all our *soul*. The Greek word translated *soul* in Matthew 22:37 is more often translated *life* in other New Testament passages. A good example is found in John 10:11: "I am the good shepherd. The good shepherd lays down his *life* for the sheep." Many of the verses which use this word have to do with giving, losing, or laying down one's life. The same word is used by Paul in his testimony before the Ephesian elders: "But none of these things move me; nor do I count my *life* dear to myself, so that I may finish my race with joy, and the ministry which I received from the Lord Jesus, to testify to the gospel of the grace of God" (Acts 20:24, *NKJV*).

In the context of Jacob's life-changing experience, let's look at what it means to love God with all our *soul*. Loving God in this way can be summarized under these three headings: a new strength of *conviction*, a new level of *commitment*, and a new depth of *consecration*.

A New Strength of Conviction

Jacob's trouble made him take a serious look at his relationship with God. He took a spiritual inventory and found that he had allowed himself and his family to drift in their conviction that Jehovah was the one true God. Pagan gods were being worshiped in his household. Some family members were doing things contrary to the will of Jehovah. The family's belief system was weak. Jacob decided to do something about it. "So Jacob said to his household and to all who were with him, 'Get rid of the foreign gods you have with you, and purify yourselves and change your clothes'" (Genesis 35:2).

Conviction can be defined as "a strong belief." One of the basic ways we demonstrate our love for God is by the strength of our convictions. The manner in which we live our lives every day is a testimony to our belief in God. How often do we allow "other gods" to dominate our decisions and our behavior? How seriously do we take God's Word as our guide in every facet of our life? Dietrich Bonhoeffer put it this way, "Only he who believes is obedient; only he who is obedient believes."

The problem in Jacob's family is the same one that permeates much of American society today. There is a nominal acceptance of Christian beliefs, but little living out of those beliefs. Other gods influence behavior, and personal holiness is relegated to the sanctimonious few. In his book, *The Frog in the Kettle*, Christian researcher George Barna, gives these observations about contemporary Christianity in America:

> Amazingly, only about one out of every five individuals say Christianity has to do with the acceptance of, or a personal relationship with Jesus Christ. Many more people

associate being a Christian with lifestyles and behavior: loving other people, helping others, being a good person, and so forth. Some equate the term with a general belief in God. . . . The concept of being a Christian has become bland and generic. Much of the spiritual dimension of the concept has been lost while the population has been immunized to the Christian faith (p. 113).

If we are to love God as we should, we must reaffirm our belief in His sovereignty and His Word. We have to stop trusting in the gods of knowledge, money, ability, popularity, and position. There can be no doubt that the lack of strong beliefs among Christians is debilitating for the church and disillusioning to the individual. The fact that there is so much moral ambiguity, spiritual lukewarmness, and gray-area-living belies the testimony of love for God.

G. Campbell Morgan noted that spiritual complacency is the worst form of blasphemy. Reports indicate that even the church is having difficulty maintaining a Scriptural standard. One major denomination recently received a study commission report that recommended the ordination of homosexuals; the approval of sex for unmarried teens, singles, and older people; and the validation of same-sex marriages.

Strong convictions seem to be out of style these days. In many cases there are no rules, no lines, no parameters, no moral absolutes. Nothing is sure. Syncretism is growing, mixing Christianity with other religious traditions. On a personal level, many could be identified as walking question marks or ones who sound like uncertain trumpets. The apostle Paul admonishes "that we should no longer be children, tossed to and fro and carried about with every wind of doctrine" (Ephesians 4:14, *NKJV*).

What we say we believe must be more than some denominational tradition, doctrinal position, or declaration of faith printed in a book. It must be a driving force that impacts all we do, 24 hours a day, seven days a week—when we are with others, and when we are alone.

Strong beliefs hold us steady in times of adversity. They motivate us to do the right things, regardless of societal trends and peer pressures. They keep us from doing the wrong things, despite multiple temptations. Deep convictions give us boldness and courage in the face of overwhelming opposition and criticism. They help us to positively influence others, our families, our friends, and even our enemies. Most importantly, strong beliefs testify to our love for God.

A New Level of Commitment

Many wonderful stories have come out of the great revival at the Brownsville Assembly of God in Pensacola, Florida. One that particularly impressed me concerned an appliance repair man (we'll call him Fred) who was set on fire by the touch of God he received. He told how he was so overcome spiritually and so wrapped up in the church services that he could not maintain his schedule of repair calls. One lady in particular got very upset with him because he had not come to take care of her appliance problem. She kept calling several times a day.

Finally Fred decided he would have to pull himself together and get back to work. The most pressing appointment seemed to be the irate lady who had called so many times.

"On my way to her house, I knew I was in trouble," Fred recalled. "The hair on my arms was standing up, and I couldn't stop crying."

Nevertheless, Fred went on. When he reached the house, he was still crying.

After checking out the problem, he found out it was something he could not fix. He tried to explain the situation to the lady, but he could not hold back the tears. The lady became even more upset.

"What in the world is wrong with you?" she demanded. "First, you take forever to get here, then you can't make the repair, and now all you can do is cry. What's going on?"

"I am so sorry, ma'am. I know this seems strange, but we have been having a revival at our church and God has touched me in a miraculous way. I apologize for acting this way, but I love God so much. I don't know what else to say."

Fred felt like he had really botched things, especially with his stumbling explanation. And the lady didn't seem to understand at all. She told him to take his "God business" and leave. But when Fred got back to his office, the telephone was ringing. It was the upset customer.

"I've been thinking," she said. "What has happened to you must be real. Could you give me the address of that church you were talking about? I want to go tonight. I've got so many problems. Maybe I can get some help."

The lady attended the service that night and gave her heart to the Lord. She testified later about how several of her family members and a number of her friends had also come to the Lord as a result of what God had done for her. The power of a life committed to God cannot be overestimated.

After Jacob got rid of the foreign Gods, purified his household, and renewed his vows to Jehovah, he put his restored faith to work. He began immediate preparation to leave for Bethel as God had commanded. He was saying in essence, "I believe God; therefore, I will obey his Word."

Unfortunately, there is too often a discrepancy in the church today between what we say we believe and how we behave. There is a trend against commitment of any kind. George Barna found that the vast majority of Americans are religious, but not committed to their beliefs. Their beliefs don't influence their actions and attitudes. They don't share their faith with others, and they are lax in Bible reading and prayer. George Gallup has stated that less than 10 percent of Americans are committed Christians.

This lack of commitment shows up also in church attendance and loyalty. It is not uncommon for a person to attend three or four churches, but be unwilling to make a commitment to any of them. Many Christians do not want to be accountable to the church or to be tied to a church job responsibility. They consistently refuse any leadership roles. Yet they would quickly tell you, "Why, of course, I love God."

The Bible clearly predicted that a lack of commitment would characterize the church in the last days.

But you must realise that in the last days the times will be full of danger. Men will become utterly self-centred, greedy for money, full of big words. They will be proud and abusive, without any regard for what their parents taught them. . . . They will be treacherous, reckless and arrogant, loving what gives them pleasure rather than loving God. They will maintain a facade of "religion" but their life denies its truth. Keep clear of people like that (2 Timothy 3:1, 2, 4, 5, *Ph.*).

God is calling the church today to make the same journey Jacob made—out of the compromising environment of secular influences, religious syncretism, and half-hearted commitment, back to a Bethel relationship with God. Bethel represented a place of spiritual intimacy and consecration. Jacob acknowledged that it was at Bethel where God appeared to him when he was fleeing from Esau.

Like any other road, the path of commitment leads from one place to another. It involves leaving, as well as arriving. Commitment means a separation from the old habits and attitudes to a new set of practical and spiritual behaviors. When we leave Shechem, as Jacob did, and arrive in Bethel, we can be sure that God will meet us there. "Therefore, come out from them and be separate, says the Lord. Touch no unclean thing, and I will receive you. I will be a Father to you, and you will be my sons and daughters, says the Lord Almighty" (2 Corinthians 6:17, 18).

This call to commitment through purity and separation is the same message given to the church at Laodicea in the Book of Revelation. Like Jacob and his family at Shechem, the people of this church thought they were doing very well, but in reality they were spiritually destitute. They lacked commitment, and they were spiritually lukewarm, neither hot nor cold. Again, like Jacob and his family, they were admonished to put on new clothes "so you can cover your shameful nakedness" (Revelation 3:18). Just as God met Jacob at Bethel, so He promised to commune with the newly committed church at Laodicea.

Loving God with all our *soul* involves a new level of commitment. God is intent on finding out if we are serious about commitment. Three times Jesus asked Peter, "Do you love me." By the third time, the Bible says Peter was offended at Jesus' persistence. It is so easy to say, "I love you." It is much more difficult to fulfill the requirements to prove it. Do you love the Lord? Do you love the Lord? Do you really love the Lord?

Then do what He is telling you to do!

A New Depth of Consecration

When my mother passed away several years ago, the Lord taught me a spiritual lesson I will never forget. Dad called to tell me that Mother was seriously ill and I should come at once if I expected to see her alive. The news was a shock to me because I had seen her just a few weeks before and she seemed to be in good health. As I flew across the country to California, I prayed that the Lord would let me see my mom alive just one more time.

When I arrived at the hospital, I could not believe my mother's physical condition. In the matter of a few weeks or so, she had wasted away to almost nothing. She was heavily sedated and appeared to be asleep. I knelt down beside her bed and began to pray. I felt so badly, seeing her in that condition. I couldn't hold back the tears.

Suddenly, the Lord spoke a message to my heart. "Don't look upon your mother's physical body. See her as she really is, perfectly whole, clothed in my righteousness, and ready to meet me." I stood up with inexpressible joy and wiped the tears from my eyes. I knew how true that message was. My mom loved the Lord with all her heart, soul, and mind. If anyone was ready to meet God, she was. I tried to visualize her in that spiritual body. What a sight!

Now I wanted to talk with her. I told her who I was and asked her if she recognized me. She opened her eyes, smiled, and spoke my name in a whisper. The cancer that ravaged her body had spread into her lungs, and she could barely speak. She tried to tell me something, but I couldn't understand. After several tries, she got frustrated. Then she began to put her hands together like she was trying to clap.

"You mean you want to sing?" I asked. She smiled and nodded in the affirmative. "What song do you want to sing?" I leaned over close to hear her answer.

"Sing, 'There Is a Fountain Filled With Blood.'"

I had sung that song many times in church, but never did it come close to having the meaning it had that day. My sister came in just at that time, and we sang together in harmony.

> There is a fountain filled with blood,
> Drawn from Immanuel's veins,
> And sinners plunged beneath that flood,
> Lose all their guilty stains. . . .
> The dying thief rejoiced to see
> That fountain in his day,
> And there may I, tho' vile as he,
> Wash all my sins away.

In a few hours Mom went to meet the Lord, vibrantly alive, sinlessly whole, dressed in the robe of His righteousness. Her consecration of many years had now reached its ultimate, glorious fulfillment.

Consecration means "to devote entirely, to give oneself to God." Consecration completes the cycle of conviction and commitment.

The first two won't hold until the last is in place. Jacob did not complete his spiritual journey until he built a new altar at Bethel. It wasn't enough to worship at the old altar, he had to build a new one to demonstrate the new depth of his consecration.

Consecration is an ongoing process. Under the Old Testament law, sacrifices had to be brought every day. The flame in the Temple never went out. This business of giving ourself to God must happen every day.

Consecration is not just a spiritual matter, it has many practical benefits as well. A recent Gallup Poll found that Christians who have "high spiritual faith" are much more able to accommodate the variables of life. They are more tolerant, less judgmental and critical. They were found to be more involved in positive ways in the church and in the community. Perhaps most noteworthy is the fact that Christians who take their faith seriously were said to be "far, far happier." We shouldn't have to rely on the Gallup Poll to tell us this truth; David said it far better over 3,000 years ago:

Blessed is the man who does not walk in the counsel of the wicked or stand in the way of sinners or sit in the seat of mockers. But his delight is in the law of the Lord, and on his law he meditates day and night. He is like a tree planted by streams of water, which yields its fruit in season and whose leaf does not wither. Whatever he does prospers (Psalm 1:1-3).

CHAPTER 5

Setting Your Mind

A preacher friend of mine was waxing eloquent in his message. Coming to a dramatic high point, he emphasized the spiritual challenge with a rhetorical question.

"I ask you," he thundered, forefinger pointed menacingly toward the congregation, "Are we mice, or are we men?"

Then, with just enough time for the impact of the question to sink in, he gave the startling answer, "I tell you, we are mice!"

Despite his quick correction of the obvious *faux pas*, his message was effectively over. His unintended point was forever fixed in the minds of his hearers.

Although this was an embarrassing moment for my friend, he was inadvertently echoing a frustration voiced by the apostle Paul, "For what I do is not the good I want to do; no, the evil I do not want to do—this I keep on doing" (Romans 7:19). Paul expressed a feeling all of us experience at times. No matter how much we set our mind to do right, we wind up doing the thing we said we would not do. Instead of being the men and women of God we desire to be, so often we act like the squeaky little mouse.

This is why Jesus' command to "love the Lord your God with all your . . . *mind*" (Luke 10:27) is so challenging. Paul gives further insight into this spiritual dilemma as he continues in Romans 7:

> For in my inner being I delight in God's law; but I see another law at work in the members of my body, waging war against the law of my mind and making me a prisoner of the law of sin at work within my members. What a wretched man I am! Who will rescue me from this body of death? Thanks be to God—through Jesus Christ our Lord! So then, I myself in my mind am a slave to God's law, but in the sinful nature a slave to the law of sin (vv. 22-25).

Loving God with our mind is different from loving God with our heart or soul. In Scripture, the word translated "mind" is used in the sense of "understanding" (Colossians 2:18), "thinking" (1 Corinthians 4:6), and "regarding" (Romans 14:6). It also has to do with the will and the intellect. It is seen as the seat of all behavior—both good and evil. The mind is the source of all we are. "For as he thinks in his heart, so is he" (Proverbs 23:7, *NKJV*).

It has been said that man lives in his head and the body is a bridge to the outside world. Every action, good and bad, has its beginning in the mind. When we understand this vital function of the mind, we can see why it is so important for the law of God to dominate and transform the mind.

The Thinking Process

Of all the creatures on earth, only man has the ability to think as we know thinking. This distinguishes him as a creation of God with the breath of God in him. This capacity to think, to contemplate, to meditate is what enables him to make choices; and this power of choice is what makes him accountable and subject to judgment. Ultimately, it is how a person utilizes the thinking process and how this in turn affects his relationships, that will determine his place in eternity.

God intended for us to use the mind, with its ability to think, in a positive way. First, we should use our mind to love God, to think on His goodness, and to exercise faith in His promises. It is a great tragedy that we so often use this wonderful gift of thought to raise doubts and fears in our mind concerning our relationship with God. Instead of simply believing his Word—that He loves us, that He forgives us, that He wants the best for us, that He is going to deliver us—we rob ourselves of the joy and release that comes from putting our trust in Him. Love implies trust, and we can't really love God unless we believe He will do what He said He will do.

We also dishonor God and violate His commandment when we use our mind to think negative thoughts about other people. This habit pattern we get into devastates us mentally and spiritually and also has a tremendous physical impact on us. I have seen this happen to other people, and I have experienced it myself. Without saying a word, a person's mental wheels start turning, and a series of negative thoughts about someone else brings on a depressive mood that can darkly color everything else that is going on. If we are to please God, we must think of others after the Spirit and not after the flesh. "So from now on we regard no one from a worldly point of view. Though we once regarded Christ in this way, we do so no longer" (2 Corinthians 5:16).

How we use the thinking process to evaluate ourself also affects our relationship with God. God is not accusatory or condemning toward us. He never puts us down. Even when we fail or disobey or sin, He still reaches out to us and promises forgiveness. As a loving Father, He will convict us and discipline us, but He will never tell us we are worthless. He wants our self-image to be strong. "For God did not give us a spirit of timidity, but a spirit of power, of love and of self-discipline" (2 Timothy 1:7). If God thinks of us and treats us as His children, to please Him we must think of ourselves in the same way.

So, thinking is the basis for all behavior. What is contemplated internally will eventually exhibit itself externally. Thought becomes action. This is why Jesus equated a lustful look with adultery. Pornography is harmful because it feeds sensual thoughts that often turn into sinful actions. Romans 1:18-32 describes this process. It is not a pretty picture. A vile imagination, a darkened understanding, a lustful thought leads to a catalog of terrible sins: greed, depravity, envy, murder, strife, deceit, malice, gossip, slander, insolence, arrogance . . . and the list goes on. It is sobering to read the results of a depraved mind.

Just as all kinds of sinful practices come from a depraved mind, so an abundance of edifying virtues flows from a renewed and transformed mind. A person who thinks good things will act out those good thoughts. As naturally as day follows night, positive thoughts produce positive actions. "Let this mind be in you, which was also in Christ Jesus" (Philippians 2:5, KJV). "Roll your works upon the Lord [commit and trust them wholly to Him; He will cause your thoughts to become agreeable to His will, and] so shall your plans be established and succeed" (Prov. 16:3, *Amp.*).

The Negative Influences

We all can identify with the apostle Paul when he described his battle to keep his thoughts in line (Romans 7). Every day we are bombarded in multiple ways with influences that run contrary to Christian principles. We have to be careful about the degree to which we are influenced by our cultural environment. That environment is becoming decidedly more anti-Christian with each passing day.

Recent reports indicate that America's cultural health is in serious decline. Former Education Secretary William Bennett, in his *Index of Leading Cultural Indicators*, says that since 1960, population, wealth, and welfare benefits have climbed, but cultural values have deteriorated.

- Violent crime has increased by 560 percent.
- Illegitimate births have climbed by 419 percent.
- Divorce rates have quadrupled.
- Teenage suicide has jumped by 200 percent.

According to Bennett, throwing money at problems won't solve them. "To turn around these numbers, we must engage in the time-honored task of the moral education of our young (and the teaching of) values such as self-restraint, respect for other people, the importance of family and self-control."

It is one thing to talk about the problems of society in general;

it is quite another thing to observe how these trends affect individuals, especially those close to us in our own family. Statistics indicate that annually 20–25 million people in America suffer from some type of mental illness. Of that number, perhaps as many as 10 million could be considered clinically depressed. Unresolved depression is the root cause for suicide. According to official reports about 30,000 people commit suicide each year in the United States. Most experts agree, however, that the real number is probably closer to 90,000 because many suicides are ruled accidental deaths.

Increasing affluence has had an adverse effect on focusing on spiritual matters and one's personal relationship with God. If nothing else, the search for riches is distracting. In light of the current emphasis on wealth in some Christian circles, it is instructive to hear again the Scriptural admonition concerning this subject:

> But godliness with contentment is great gain. For we brought nothing into the world, and we can take nothing out of it. But if we have food and clothing, we will be content with that. People who want to get rich fall into temptation and a trap and into many foolish and harmful desires that plunge men into ruin and destruction. For the love of money is a root of all kinds of evil. Some people, eager for money, have wandered from the faith and pierced themselves with many griefs (1 Timothy 6:6-10).

It is not a sin to be rich, but the Bible condemns the love of money and the pursuit of wealth. Unfortunately, many Christians are failing to heed God's warnings concerning the love of money. A misinterpretation of 3 John 2, "Dear friend, I pray that you may enjoy good health and that all may go well with you, even as your soul is getting along well," has caused many believers to focus on getting wealth and has distracted them from their primary responsibility of loving God. When our mind is on money, it is difficult to keep our spiritual priorities straight.

The influence of television and other forms of entertainment has had a dramatic impact on the attitudes and actions of people generally. This is also true for Christians. The erosion of moral values has been no less evident among Christians than among the population at large. We cannot be constantly exposed to television, videos, compact discs, and the internet without being negatively influenced. These spiritually destructive forces can be minimized only through proper controls.

Satan himself is the agent behind all of these negative influences. The Bible calls him "the prince of the power of the air" (Ephesians 2:2, KJV) and "the prince of this world" (John 16:11). It is not coincidental that the air waves disseminate so much of the cultural trash. In a personal sense, we are most vulnerable to the devices of the devil in our thinking processes. The mind is his realm of operation. "The god of this age has blinded the minds of unbelievers, so that they cannot see the light of the gospel of the glory of Christ, who is the image of God" (2 Corinthians 4:4).

We must admit that these negative influences can deter us from the goal of loving God as we should. The mind is the area most susceptible to Satan's attacks. This is why loving God with all our *mind* is so important. The mind is like a sponge. It absorbs the influences around it. If it is filled with one substance, however, it will not absorb another. Fill a sponge with oil, drop it into a pail of water, and the water will not affect the sponge.

When we are filled with the Spirit of God, the negative elements of our cultural environment will have little effect on us. "Do not get drunk on wine, which leads to debauchery. Instead, be filled with the Spirit" (Ephesians 5:18).

The Spiritual Solution

God created our thinking process. He intended for it to function properly so that we could know and understand Him and thus love Him for who He is. He also gave us cognitive ability so we could know others in the right way and love them as He loves us. He wants us to use our mind to think straight about ourself. In other words, God endowed us with the capacity to think in order to facilitate our relationships at all three levels: with God, others, and self.

When our mind is "messed up," when it is blinded, depressed, or corrupted, we cannot think as God intended. If this happens, God says he will clear our mind and open our understanding. He will give us the mind of Christ. He will deliver us from the oppression of the devil.

This was demonstrated to me forcefully through an experience I had as a pastor. One day I was praying, and the Lord gave me a strong impression that one of the ladies in the church was bound by addiction to cigarettes. This was puzzling because this lady, Shirley, was one of the best members, an active church supporter, and a Sunday school teacher. The more I tried to put the matter out of my mind, the stronger the impression became. I knew I had to confront the issue with her.

A few days later, my wife and I went to see Shirley when we knew she would be home alone. I reluctantly broached the subject with her and was surprised when she immediately broke into tears.

"Pastor," she said, "I know the Lord had to reveal this to you because no one in the world knows I have this problem, not even my husband and children. I have hidden it for years, and the devil has told me every day what a terrible hypocrite I am. Lately, it has gotten worse. I feel like I'm on the verge of a nervous breakdown. But I've been praying . . . " She was so emotionally overwhelmed, she couldn't continue.

I assured her that God understood how she felt and that He didn't condemn her. That was the reason He let me know what her problem was. He wanted to deliver her, not just from the addiction to cigarettes, but more importantly from the mental oppression that perpetuated the problem.

We had a wonderful prayer together, and I thought the spiritual work had been done. But Shirley called me the next day, very discouraged. She still had her problem. I encouraged her to keep praying and to keep resisting the devil, especially as he came against her mentally.

As I stepped to the pulpit to preach the following Sunday, I looked across the congregation and saw Shirley. Tears were streaming down her cheeks. I knew this was God's time. I asked the congregation to stand for prayer, and without another word, I walked off the platform and down the side aisle to the back of the church where Shirley and her family stood. When she saw me coming, she raised both her hands and began to rejoice. Before I could get to her to pray, she was already delivered—forever!

I believed then and still believe that Shirley's problem was not cigarettes, but the mental prison Satan had put her in. The mind-battles we fight manifest themselves in different ways. If the devil can bind us mentally, he knows we are easy targets for other arrows of destruction. But God has promised us authority over every power of the devil. "The Spirit in you is far stronger than anything in the world" (1 John 4:4, *The Message*).

Of the miracles Jesus performed, 26 refer to the healing of the mind as well as of the body. In the beautiful story of the deliverance of the Gadarene demoniac, people came to see the former wild man and found him "sitting at Jesus' feet, dressed and in his right mind" (Luke 8:35). That is what God wants for every one of His children. It is His will that we have our right mind—thinking clearly and creatively, understanding God, others, and ourself.

When we love God with our mind, Christ takes control of our thinking, and He sanctifies our thoughts. He gives us pure thoughts, good thoughts, joyful thoughts, creative thoughts. Not only does the Lord sanctify our thoughts, but he also sensitizes them. We will be more aware of what is going on with other people. We will be more understanding and accepting of them. We will pay closer attention to what is happening in our family and in other relationships. We will perceive people and situations differently.

When we have the mind of Christ, we are better able to cope with the complexities of life. He clarifies our vision, calms our fears, and gives us peace of mind. To receive these benefits, however, it is necessary for us to fulfill certain important responsibilities.

The Human Response

One of the most important truths taught in the Bible is the principle of the responsibility of choice. As noted earlier, the ability to choose implies the necessity of accountability. A classic illustration of this principle is found in Joshua 24:15. Joshua challenged the children of Israel: "But if serving the Lord seems undesirable to you, then choose for yourselves this day whom you will serve, whether the gods your forefathers served beyond the River, or the gods of the Amorites, in whose land you are living. But as for me and my household, we will serve the Lord."

Nowhere is this principle of choice more relevant than in the cognitive realm, in the mind. Again and again in Scripture we are given commands concerning making the right choices in our thinking. We are told to think on the good things (Philippians 4:8). We are to have the mind of Christ (Philippians 2:5). Our mind is to be renewed and transformed (Romans 12:2). We do have control over what we think. We can make choices as to the course of our thoughts. And the choices we make determine the actions we take.

Remember Joseph's brothers? It is hard to imagine that grown men could take their anger out on a teenage brother to the degree that they would contemplate killing him, finally deciding to sell him into slavery. Their action was not a spur-of-the-moment decision. It had been brewing for a long time. It had been percolating in their minds. First, they envied and were jealous of him. Then they began to hate him, and when the time came, they conspired against him. That led to throwing him in a pit and eventually selling him to slave traders. Their long-term negative thinking toward Joseph would have caused them to kill him if one brother hadn't intervened.

Thinking follows a programmed pattern. That pattern is fixed in each of us through our family background, our cultural environment, and sometimes through certain traumatic events in our life. But the most critical factor is our spiritual inheritance, both good and evil. We are all born in sin, and our thinking is influenced by this fact in basic ways. However, when we give our heart to God, he provides a whole new pattern of thinking which is in line with his will and purpose. The problem is that the new way of thinking is not automatic. We have to choose the new pattern, and it must be done on a continuing basis because of the intervening negative influences.

We can think right! We can stop thinking wrong! We can break those patterns which keep making us do things that hurt ourself and others. We can love the Lord with all our mind. It may not be easy, but it is possible. And God will always be there to help us. The secret is to let Him.

> Just as I am, poor, wretched, blind;
>> Sight, riches, healing of the mind,
> Yea, all I need in Thee to find,
>> O Lamb of God, I come! I come!

CHAPTER 6

Practicing
Your
Worship

In previous chapters, we looked at the three levels of loving God that Jesus talked about in Matthew 22:37: loving Him with all your *heart*, with all your *soul*, and with all your *mind*. The original Old Testament reference (Deuteronomy 6:5), as well as other New Testament passages (Mark 12:30 and Luke 10:27), add the word *strength* to the list.

This chapter focuses on that fourth way of loving God: "with all your *strength*." The Greek word for strength is also translated *power, might,* and *ability* in other New Testament passages. For our purposes in this chapter, *strength* will refer to the power, might and ability to love God by worshiping Him through Scriptural behavior.

The key to our discussion are the guidelines set in Romans 12:1, 2; however we will look at the entire chapter in the course of our study. The scripture is a familiar passage, but it takes on new meaning through this translation by J.B. Phillips:

With eyes wide open to the mercies of God, I beg you, my brothers, as an act of intelligent worship, to give him your bodies, as a living sacrifice, consecrated to him and acceptable by him. Don't let the world around you squeeze you into its own mould, but let God re-make you so that your whole attitude of mind is changed.

According to this passage, we are to present ourselves to God "as an act of intelligent worship." What better way to love God, what better way to worship God, than to consecrate and dedicate ourself to him? The important point here is that our worship, our consecration, is to be brought to the Lord in the form of Scriptural behavior. Living every day according to God's law is our "act of intelligent worship." The rest of Romans 12 outlines this kind of behavior. The only way we can meet the Lord's standard of behavior is to "let God re-make [us] so that [our] whole attitude of mind is changed."

The Worship Debate

It must grieve the heart of God to see His people embroiled in a debate over styles of worship. This is happening in many Christian circles today. Often the debate becomes more than a discussion and erupts into an open controversy.

Some feel that praise should be given preeminence in the worship service; others say the emphasis should be on preaching. Some love to sing choruses (lots of choruses!); others feel that only the traditional hymns are appropriate. Some sing from words projected on a screen; others think that is a desecration of the hymn book. Some like their music slow and soft; others can only be blessed if it is loud and fast. Some lift hands, clap hands, hold hands; others don't think hands should be used in worship at all. Some believe in silent prayer; others prefer concert prayer; still others think one should pray for all. And the list goes on.

There are no set formulas or pat answers to questions about worship. It is doubtful that God has much concern about the styles or mechanics of worship. What does break his heart are the divisions in His body caused by disagreements over worship.

While we may not know how to resolve all the conflicts, some things about worship we know for certain.

• We know God *deserves* our worship. He is worthy of our praise, honor, adoration, and blessing.

• We know God *desires* our worship. Psalm 22 tells that He inhabits the praises of his people.

• We know also that God *directs* our worship. He mandates that those who worship Him must worship Him in spirit (knowledge) and in truth (commitment).

Intelligent, rational, spiritual worship involves two basic concepts: a knowledge of God and a commitment to God. If we are to love God with all our *strength*, we must seek to know Him and then to give ourself to Him.

Understanding God's Person

Paul admonishes us to keep our eyes wide open. We must at all times be seeking to know more about God. When a man is in love, he wants to know all he can about the object of his affection. He wants to be around her. He is interested in everything about her. He listens carefully to her every word. She is at the center of his universe.

81

The same is true of our relationship with God. If we love God, we want to know more about Him. We want to draw closer to Him. But so many things come up in the daily course of life to take our attention away from Him! We must make a conscious effort every waking moment to keep God on our mind and in our heart. That is what it means to "pray without ceasing." We can commune with God in the midst of the busiest day.

I heard about a mother with many children, always underfoot, competing for her attention. She never had a free moment. Someone asked her how she ever had time to pray. "When things get too hectic," she said, "I just throw my apron over my head, and the Lord and I have our own little sanctuary." All of us need to use our apron like that from time to time.

If we truly love God, we will focus on Him at all times. In worship He will be the central attraction. When we understand that we come to the house of God to meet Him and to worship Him, we will not be so concerned about the other elements of the worship service. It will not matter so much who the preacher is or what songs are sung or what the style of worship is. Our interest and concern will center on one thing: worshiping the Lord in spirit and in truth.

When Isaiah went to the Temple in Isaiah 6, he had one goal in mind—to meet the Lord. He was not disappointed. He saw the Lord high and lifted up. Smoke filled the Temple. The pillars began to quake. Isaiah had a life-changing experience because he had an encounter with God.

Our worship experiences don't usually match Isaiah's because we don't have the focus he did. We don't set the same worship priorities. We are too easily distracted by any number of minor things. We depend too much on our own feelings. One thing we do know: if we will make an effort—even a feeble effort—to seek God, we will find Him. He has promised that. If we will hear His gentle knock at the door of our heart and open the door even the slightest bit, He will come in and touch us and forgive us and deliver us—just as He did Isaiah.

The first step to worshiping God in spirit and truth is focusing on Him to the exclusion of any other less important things.

Understanding God's Power

To love God as we should, we must not only understand who He is (His person), but we must also remember what He has done (His power). This is why God commanded Israel to keep the Passover. He wanted them to be reminded on a regular basis of His miracles in delivering them from Egypt. This is also the reason the Lord instituted the sacrament of Communion to be celebrated in remembrance of Him.

To count our blessings enhances our worship experience because it puts the focus where it should be—on the Lord. It creates in us the proper attitude for worship—gratitude and faith. Acknowledging the reality of God's power in our life gives our spirit an immediate boost and helps us not to be so self-centered, worrying about our own problems and failing to give glory to God.

When I am down in my own life and my priorities start getting out of line, I have a ritual that never fails to get me refocused spiritually.

When I was first called into the ministry at age 19, I had several tough experiences that really "knocked me for a loop." Besides an auto accident, financial woes, and courtship struggles, I developed cancer in my right foot which eventually spread up my leg and into my thigh. By the time the cancer was discovered, it had become life-threatening. With no resources and very little faith, I was devastated. But the Lord who had called me into the ministry had mercy on me and used an evangelist named Oral Roberts to bring a miraculous healing. Within two years the Lord delivered me out of all my troubles. He gave me a brand-new car, a brand-new wife, and a brand-new lease on life.

That wonderful deliverance did not solve all my problems or supply all my needs, but what it did do was give me an assurance that my God is with me and will never leave me nor forsake me. So when my faith gets low and I need to remember why I love the Lord so much, I go back to that watershed moment in my life and rejoice again in the blessings of God. It works every time.

This idea of remembering what God has done is solidly grounded in the Scriptures. It is more than a good idea, it is a divine command. "Remember the wonders he has done, his miracles, and the judgments he pronounced" (Psalm 105:5).

In our relationship with God, we must always keep in mind that it is not what we can do, but what He can do that will make the ultimate difference in life and ministry.

Understanding God's Promise

Another important facet of our knowledge of God is not just what He has done, but also what He is going to do. The Bible is full of promises made by God to His people. Many of these promises have already been fulfilled, which is one of the undeniable proofs of the authenticity of the Bible. Many more of these promises are yet to be fulfilled, which provide great hope and excitement for the Christian. The fact that an incredible number of God's promises have already come to pass strengthens the faith of God's people to believe that ultimately every promise will be fulfilled.

When we understand that Almighty God is not only a maker of promises, but also a keeper of promises, it increases our love for Him. Because God loves us, He has made us many wonderful promises. A number of these promises have to do with our life on earth. They deal with the realities of life, recognizing that the people of God will experience both good times and bad times.

Just before Jesus went to the cross, He had a long talk with His disciples, letting them know what was going to happen to them in the future. The record of what Jesus said to the disciples on this occasion can be found in John 13–17. These three chapters are filled with instructions, admonitions, warnings, prayers, and promises. It is the most extensive continuous historical record of the words of Jesus found in the Bible.

When Jesus spoke to the disciples about their lives after He returned to the Father, He did not mince words. He gave them the bad news as well as the good news. He let them know that they would be hated and persecuted. Some of them would even die for the sake of the gospel. "They will put you out of the synagogue; in fact, a time is coming when anyone who kills you will think he is offering a service to God" (John 16:2).

Even though Jesus issued these strong warnings, the heart of His message was a promise of peace and victory. One of the most wonderful promises in the Bible was made by Jesus during this discourse: "Peace I leave with you; my peace I give you. I do not give to you as the world gives. Do not let your hearts be troubled and do not be afraid" (John 14:27). Probably the best summary of Jesus' words is found in John 16:33: "These things I have spoken to you, that in Me you may have peace. In the world you will have tribulation; but be of good cheer, I have overcome the world" (*NKJV*).

As Christians, we are grateful for the assurance we have of God's peace and victory in this present world. However, an even greater sense of joy comes from the knowledge that the promises of God extend to the world to come. In this same passage Jesus gave perhaps the most precious promise of all:

> Let not your heart be troubled; you believe in God, believe also in me. In my Father's house are many mansions; if it were not so, I would have told you. I go to prepare a place for you. And if I go and prepare a place for you, I will come again and receive you to Myself; that where I am, there you may be also. (John 14:1-3, *NKJV*).

Growing in Worship

The Christian life is a progressive walk. We should be maturing, moving, and pressing toward the mark. We should be growing up (and be children no longer) in our relationship with God. One of the vital areas of maturation is in our worship. We should be moving on in our worship from a knowledge of God to a commitment to God. A knowledge of God is not just to inform, but to reform and transform. The better we know God the more we should love Him and the more committed to Him we should be. According to Romans 12 we have an obligation to present ourself as a living sacrifice, and to "let God re-make [our] . . . whole attitude" (v. 2, *Ph.*). This is an ongoing process.

As we move on in our worship, we will experience a maturing

change, hopefully even a transformation. Here are some areas to consider as we progress in worship, understanding that we do not have to leave one area to grow to another:

- Grow from spirit to truth—adding obedience to blessing.
- Grow from privilege to duty—accepting spiritual responsibility.
- Grow from faith to works—believing produces action.
- Grow from hearing to doing—bringing a behavioral change.
- Grow from church to home—making home a sanctuary.
- Grow from the sanctuary to the streets—taking worship to the marketplace.
- Grow from Sunday to Monday—making every day a worship day.
- Grow from feast to sacrifice—adding dedication to jubilation.

A Change in Attitude

Growth brings change. After Paul talks about engaging in "intelligent worship" through the giving of ourself in dedication as a living sacrifice, he challenges us to make some significant behavioral changes. These changes begin in the transformation of our attitude. The first two verses of Romans 12 lay down the challenge of practicing our worship through behavioral change, and the next 19 verses demonstrate in a practical way what it meant by this concept.

Notice these specific admonitions concerning attitude.

- Don't have an exaggerated opinion of yourself (v. 3).
- Practice love without hypocrisy (v. 9).
- Be devoted to (have warm affection for) one another (v. 10).

- Let others take the credit (v. 10).
- Endure trials patiently (v. 12).
- Don't be snobbish (v. 16).
- Don't be dogmatic (v. 16).

What Paul is pleading for is an attitude that extends worship to everyday living. He is saying that a dominating attitude toward family members on the way home from church or a mean spirit toward a waitress at a meal after church is totally unacceptable. A prideful, conceited, hard-hearted, snobbish, dogmatic attitude nullifies our worship and discredits our testimony. A Christian with a transformed attitude will demonstrate sincerity, humility, kindness, and courtesy.

And these are just the verses on attitude. There are two more areas to go.

A Change in Action

When Jesus ministered to the woman at the well (John 4), He told her that the specific place of worship was not as important as the attitude and behavior of the worshiper. "Believe me, woman, a time is coming when you will worship the Father neither on this mountain nor in Jerusalem. . . . Yet a time is coming and has now come when the true worshipers will worship the Father in spirit and truth" (vv. 21, 23).

Romans 12 amplifies this teaching by saying that intelligent or "spiritual" worship doesn't necessarily happen in the synagogue or on a particular day of the week, but it boils down to a lifestyle. He refers to certain practical actions that are characteristic of the Christian.

Verse 11 refers to diligence and zeal in our work. J.B. Phillips translates the first part of verse 11: "Let us not allow slackness to spoil our work." *The Living Bible* renders the verse: "Never be lazy in your work but serve the Lord enthusiastically." We need to remember the importance of doing a good job and not being lazy. The seven dwarfs of Snow White fame sang "Whistle While You Work." An appropriate song for a follower of Christ could be "Worship While You Work."

Another practical way to worship the Lord and demonstrate our love for Him and others is indicated in verse 13: "Share with God's people who are in need. Practice hospitality." Jesus indicated that a cup of cold water could have eternal implications. If we lift a hand on Sunday, we need to lend a hand on Monday.

One more verse to illustrate the need for practical action: "Do things in such a way that everyone can see you are honest clear through" (v. 17, *TLB*). Public behavior that is above reproach brings glory and honor to Christ.

A Change in Association

The spiritual transformation Paul is calling for extends to our relationships. Although it wasn't planned this way, this final section on loving God—with all our strength—leads beautifully into Part II of this book, "Loving Others." Paul gives us a number of verses that talk specifically about our responsibility to certain kinds of people: enemies, those who are happy, those who are hurting, ordinary people, and troublemakers.

Here are five people-pleasing rules:

- Bless those who mistreat you. Don't curse them (v. 14).
- Be happy with those who are happy; be sad with those who are sad (v. 15).

- Take a real interest in ordinary people (v. 16).
- As far as your responsibility goes, live at peace with everyone (v. 18).
- Don't take revenge on anyone; leave that to God (v. 19).

True worship involves our relationship with others which, in turn, affects our relationship with God. In fact, every person we come in contact with influences in some way our relationship with God. There is no doubt that many Christians are bound in their worship because of their poor relations with others. In some cases, God will not hear our prayers or accept our worship gifts if there is a relationship problem.

> Therefore, if you are offering your gift at the altar and there remember that your brother has something against you, leave your gift there in front of the altar. First go and be reconciled to your brother; then come and offer your gift (Matthew 5:23, 24).

The greatest commandment of all states: "Love the Lord your God with all your heart and with all your soul and with all your strength and with all your mind" (Luke 10:27). When that relationship is right, it powerfully and positively affects relationships at every other level.

PART 2

Loving Others

✳ ✳ ✳

Dear friends,
let us love one another,
for love comes from God.

1 John 4:7

CHAPTER 7

The Heart of the Message

J esus said that loving God is man's most important responsibility. Following hard on the heels of that commandment, however, is man's second most important responsibility: loving others. While Jesus talked a lot about our relationship with God, He talked more about our relationship with others. One of His earliest teachings, the Sermon on the Mount, dealt almost entirely with interpersonal relationships. His last major message before going to the cross focused on loving others (John 13–17). "My command is this: Love each other as I have loved you" (15:12).

Demonstrated by Jesus

"Whatever you want your children to be, be that first yourselves." That is a true saying; we teach best by example. Jesus understood this better than anyone. Everything He did was calculated to drive home some principle of truth. One day His disciples were having a dispute because the mother of James and John had asked Him to give her two sons a place of prominence in His kingdom. That request sparked a big discussion about power and position. Jesus used the occasion to give them one of His most important teachings:

> You know that the rulers of the Gentiles lord it over them, and their high officials exercise authority over them. Not so with you. Instead, whoever wants to become great among you must be your servant, and whoever wants to be first must be your slave (Matthew 20:25-27).

Jesus continued, "Just as the Son of Man did not come to be served, but to serve, and to give his life a ransom for many" (v. 28). He taught a whole new way of relating to others by powerfully demonstrating the truths through His own life. He related in a positive, serving way to every person He came in contact with.

One of the earliest teaching encounters Jesus had was with a woman at Jacob's well (John 4). In this meeting, He demonstrated several important interpersonal principles.

He gave personal attention. He went out of his way to meet one-on-one with this woman. His focus on her and her needs spoke loudly of how much He valued her as an individual. His attention raised the woman's self-esteem and gave her hope.

He showed a total lack of prejudice. He was willing to associate with someone His peers considered racially inferior. The Jews had no dealings with the Samaritans. He also made no difference because she was a woman. Jesus was continually elevating the status of women.

He demonstrated a nonjudgmental attitude. Even though He knew ahead of time that she was a social outcast, a divorcee, and one who was living in sin, He met with her and forgave her. While He did not judge or condemn her, He did confront her so that conviction could bring her to repentance.

He had a teaching spirit. He took time with her and answered her questions. He listened to her opinions and explanations, but then did not hesitate to give her God's truth which produced in her a personal joy and a boldness to witness.

In His behavior toward other people, Jesus portrayed the fruit of the Spirit. He was kind, courteous, and understanding. He was compassionate. "When he saw the crowds, he had compassion on them, because they were harassed and helpless, like sheep without a shepherd" (Matthew 9:36). He extended mercy, as in the case of the woman taken in adultery. He said, "Then neither do I condemn you. . . . Go now and leave your life of sin" (John 8:11).

He was sensitive. When others rebuked the blind man, He called for him and healed him. Jesus paid attention to children. When the woman with the issue of blood touched Him, He sensed it. Even while He was suffering and dying on the cross, He was sensitive to the needs of His mother and asked John to care for her. He blessed people wherever He went.

On the other hand, He was not always "Mr. Nice Guy." When it was necessary, He could be confrontational and a disciplinarian, as He was with the Pharisees and Sadducees. He was candid and honest, as shown in His response to the rich young ruler. He could also be pointed with friends, as He was with Martha.

A prime example of the way Jesus viewed human relationships occurred just before the Crucifixion. He put on a towel and washed the disciples' feet. Then He said to them: "I have set you an example that you should do as I have done for you" (John 13:15). Of course, the greatest demonstration of His love for others came when Jesus went to the cross. "Greater love has no one than this, that he lay down his life for his friends" (15:13).

Jesus is our model when it comes to loving others. Whenever a question arises concerning our responsibility to others, we have but to respond, "What would Jesus do?" When we discover the answer to that question, then we must act accordingly. We must do as He did!

Demanded of His Followers

If there is any place in Scripture where God draws a hard and fast line, it is in the connection between loving God and loving others. His command is very clear and there is no flexibility. How strongly does God feel about this matter? Check out this scripture:

> If anyone says, "I love God," yet hates his brother, he is a liar. For anyone who does not love his brother, whom he has seen, cannot love God, whom he has not seen. And he has given us this command: Whoever loves God must also love his brother (1 John 4:20, 21).

Recently I had the privilege of visiting the country of Vietnam. I had never been there before, so I was quite anxious to go. I had mixed feelings, however, because the country is still under tight Communist control and they do not look kindly on visiting church leaders from America. In fact, I received word the day before I left that Vietnamese officials had just arrested a church leader visiting from America.

I had been instructed by those who had invited me about how

to clear customs and where to meet my contact once I had left the airport. The purpose of my visit was to meet with some underground church leaders. I did not realize until after I got there what a risk those leaders were taking by inviting me to come.

I made it through customs without any apparent difficulty and found the place where I was to be picked up. To my surprise, in a few minutes a young Vietnamese man pulled up on a motorbike. He apologized for not having better transportation and asked me if I would mind riding on the back of the bike. I jumped on and we were off for one of the most incredible journeys of my life.

As we sped through the streets of Ho Chi Minh City (former Saigon), with thousands of bikes, carts, and scooters coming at us, it seemed, from all directions, I heard the unbelievable testimony of the young pastor who was my driver. He told me how he had been arrested, jailed, and tortured many times because he was a Christian and especially because he was a pastor. Only a few weeks before, he was teaching a group of his people in a secret area when the authorities were heard next door. His people told him to run so he would not be arrested again, but he refused. One more time, he was taken to jail and grilled by the officials. He was threatened and released. He didn't know how long he could remain free.

I asked this earnest young preacher how he could continue under such dangerous circumstances. I will never forget his answer. He turned toward me and I could see the tears glistening on his cheeks. "I have no fear," he said, "because I love God and I love my people more than I love my own life."

For months after I returned from Vietnam, I could still see the face of that young man and hear his vibrant testimony. I wondered in my heart if I were in his place, could I make the kind of commitment he has made. I wondered if the affluent church in America really understands the implications of Jesus' words, "Love one another as I have loved you."

Jesus' teaching concerning relationships was a radical departure from the Old Testament rules. In the Sermon on the Mount (see Matthew 5), He stated several times, "You have heard it said . . . but I say." Every one of the new commandments given by Jesus have to do with our relationships with others:

Old Statement	New Statement
• Don't commit murder.	• Don't be angry with your brother without cause.
• Don't commit adultery	• Don't look upon a woman with lust in your heart.
• Divorce for any cause.	• No divorce except for sexual immorality.
• Don't swear falsely.	• Don't swear at all.
• An eye for an eye; a tooth for a tooth.	• Turn the other cheek; go the second mile.
• Hate your enemy.	• Love your enemy.

The thread that runs through the Sermon on the Mount, beginning with the Beatitudes, is "Do what is right and problems with others and deficiencies in life will take care of themselves." Not only should we not worry with these problems, but we are actually to rejoice and be happy. "And what happiness will be yours when people blame you and ill-treat you and say all kinds of slanderous things against you for my sake! Be glad then, yes, be tremendously glad—for your reward in Heaven is magnificent" (Matthew 5:11, 12, *Ph.*).

Later in this book we will be discussing the idea of actually finding joy in your relationships with your enemies, but it might be well at this point to note that the concepts of happiness and joy permeate Jesus' teachings concerning relationships. In the Beatitudes, where the theme is definitely negative concerning needs, the command is extremely positive with regard to attitude. The King James Version and various other translations use the term *blessed* at the beginning of each beatitude but there are other translations that use the word *happy*. However, most Bible scholars would agree that neither word is quite strong enough to convey the meaning in the original Greek. A more literal translation would be something like "How lucky you are!"

We don't feel very lucky sometimes when life is dealing us bitter blows and our relationships seem to be going in reverse. But the paradox of the gospel is that "the first shall be last and the last shall be first" and that "he who loses his life shall find it."

Phillip Yancey, in his book *The Jesus I Never Knew*, offers some wonderful insights on this idea:

> In the Beatitudes, strange sayings that at first glance seem absurd, Jesus offers a paradoxical key to abundant life. The kingdom of heaven, He said elsewhere, is of such value that any shrewd investor would "in his joy" sell all he has in order to buy it. It represents value far more real and permanent than anything the world has to offer, for this treasure will pay dividends both here on earth and also in the life to come. Jesus places emphasis not on what we give up

but on what we receive. Is it not in our own self-interest to pursue such a treasure? (p. 125)

The way Jesus taught and lived with regard to interpersonal relationships is not a burden for the Christian to bear, but a blessing to share. But we must never forget that these teachings of Jesus are not merely suggestions to consider, they are commands to obey. In fact, the quality of life here on earth and our place in eternity will be determined by how well we obey these commands.

Defined in Judgment

So the Great Commandment, along with numerous other passages of Scripture, teaches us that we are not only to love God but we are to love our neighbor as we love ourselves. The Scriptural principle states that if we truly love God, we will love others. How we relate to God determines how we will relate to others.

The reverse of this principle is also true. How we relate to others will determine how we relate to God.

The truth of this latter principle is particularly relevant when seen in the context of the final judgment. Matthew 25:31–46 describes the standards by which God will judge the nations. These standards have to do with practical relationships. Verses 41-43 state:

> Then I will turn to those on my left and say, "Away with you, you cursed ones, into the eternal fire prepared for the devil and his demons. For I was hungry and you wouldn't feed me; thirsty and you wouldn't give me anything to drink; a stranger, and you refused me hospitality; naked, and you wouldn't clothe me; sick, and in prison, and you didn't visit me" (TLB).

What this passage tells us is that our place in eternity depends on the quality of our relationships. Our failure to live up to God's standards in interpersonal behavior is much more serious than an attitude problem or a personality flaw. According to the words of Jesus, that failure could have eternal consequences.

It is clear that the above scriptures apply to programs of social action. However, God is referring to more than hospital and prison ministries. He is talking about more than just the poor and the homeless. While these ministries are important, the subject here is much more personal and practical. Many people are hungry and thirsty for much more than food and water. More than physical shelter is needed by those who feel left out and shut out. Clothing won't cover the nakedness of the psychologically and spiritually destitute. A visit won't cure someone bound in a prison of doubt, fear, and anxiety.

The matter boils down to whether we understand the seriousness of our responsibilities to those around us, and whether we are willing to fulfill those responsibilities. Our job begins with those closest to us—the members of our own family—and extends as far as our influence reaches. If you are married, your relationship with your spouse supersedes every other obligation you have. If you have children, they are next in line, above everyone and everything else. Other relationship responsibilities fall in line behind these.

Romans 14:12 states, "So then, each of us will give account of himself to God." Understanding that personal judgment is inevitable and that personal relationships, with God and with others, will determine the outcome of that judgment—what manner of person ought we to be in the fruit we bear?

CHAPTER 8

The Attitude of Joy

D r. Sunshine. That is what people called my grandmother during the latter years of her life. I remember as a little boy how fascinated I was every time I went to visit her. Her house was like a disorganized library. Books and pamphlets and gospel tracts everywhere. But the thing I remember most was the large map of the United States that hung on her living room wall. It was covered with black, red, and white pins.

Grandmother was a widow for the last 30 years of her life. My grandfather, Elmer K. Fisher, a prominent leader of the early pentecostal movement, died in a flu epidemic at a relatively young age. After his death, my grandmother began to develop a unique ministry of her own. She would get the name and address of a person who was not a Christian. Usually it was the name of a loved one given to her by a family member who had been praying for that person's salvation.

My grandmother would start corresponding with that person,

usually sending along a poem or an excerpt from a book. Always she would enclose a tract of some kind. Her letters were chatty and uplifting, never preachy. Amazingly, most people would write back and a friendship by mail would begin to develop.

Every time she started corresponding with a new person, Grandmother would place a black pin on the map, in the city where that person lived. Over a period of time, as she prayed and kept corresponding with the person, she would get the wonderful news that her pen pal had become a Christian. When that happened, she replaced the black pin with a red one, signifying that the blood of Jesus had done its work in another heart. But she didn't stop there. She kept up the correspondence and sent along helpful teaching material for the new Christian. When she felt the person had finally become strong in the faith, she would replace the red pin with a white one.

I am still amazed when I think of the incredible influence of this lady. She lived alone on meager funds, but she had a burning passion to see lives changed by the power of God. In my mind I can still see that big map with its hundreds of black, red, and white pins. What a monument to the positive influence of one joyful life. I love what you taught me, Dr. Sunshine!

The most edifying thing we can do for others is to have a loving, joyful relationship with them. To affirm a person—to be kind, courteous, and appreciative—has an impact that will last a lifetime and extend to eternity. And it costs so little. On the other hand, the most damaging, devastating thing we can do is to allow a relationship to become negative, critical, and bitter.

Some time ago I was asked to participate in the funeral of a man who had a history of negative relationships. As I looked over the audience, I knew many of them were there not because of their affinity for the man in the casket, but out of respect to his family. Sadly, the thoughts of many that day did not focus on any good things the man had done, but tragically on painful remembrances of past negative personal encounters. Wounds from interpersonal battles do not heal quickly. Scars remain for a lifetime.

It is doubtful that most of us understand the awesome power we wield in our relationships with others and how much those relationships impact us. Much of what we think of ourselves is determined by how we perceive others view us. Just a smile, even a slight smile, from another person can lift our spirit sometimes for days. That smile says, "I like you. You are a worthwhile person." Likewise, a frown or a lack of attention says, "I don't like you. You have no worth to me."

We are sensitive to what others think of us—often overly sensitive. We are always looking and watching for the reaction of others. This sensitivity may pose a problem at times, but it also provides a wonderful opportunity. Sometimes a simple positive word or gesture can turn a life around. Mark Twain said, "I can live for two months on a sincere compliment." One loving, joyful person can change a lot of people for the better. And the more intimate the relationship, the greater the difference made.

Joyful in Relationship With Family

Listen to all the joy in this description of family relationships:

The father of the righteous will greatly rejoice, and he who begets a wise child will delight in him. Let your father and your mother be glad, and let her who bore you rejoice (Proverbs 23:24, 25, NKJV).

Happiness begins at home. Our greatest joys and deepest sorrows come from family relationships. In the home, we are physically closer to one another. We are more emotionally involved, we spend more time together, we know more about each other—good and bad. It is only natural that relationships in this kind of setting are more impactful.

God wants all relationships to be joyful, especially in the family. On the other hand, the devil does all he can to bring division and unhappiness to the family. He knows that if things are not right in the family, they will not be right anywhere else—in the school, on the job, in the church, and in society in general. But if things are right in the family, usually they will be right everywhere else.

The best investment of time and energy in relationships, then, ought to be with the family. One of the biggest problems in the family is that we tend to become set in our habit patterns. Even though we know a certain behavior gets us into trouble every time with another family member, we continue to practice that behavior because it's a habit and we can't think of a better alternative. The truth is, a conscious change to a better, more Scriptural behavior pattern can absolutely transform a relationship.

A couple on the verge of divorce once came to me for counseling. They both stated that they were unhappy in the marriage and that their relationship had become virtually meaningless. The wife described her boring life:

Here's the way a typical day goes. My husband gets up early and goes to work. He comes home at precisely 5:30 in the afternoon. I can set my clock by it. When he gets home, he never comes in the front door, always the back door. And if I am anywhere around, he does his best to avoid me. He takes a shower, changes his clothes, reads the newspaper, and watches TV until I call him for supper. He sits down at the table, gobbles up his food without comment, and then goes back to his chair to watch TV. In a couple of hours, he's nodding off and I suggest he go to bed. He stumbles down the hallway, falls into bed, and his snoring is the last I hear from him until the next morning. It's such a boring life. I can't put up with it anymore.

The husband was eager to tell his side of the story:

Let me tell you how I see it. I work hard every day. Yes, I do come home right at 5:30 p.m. At least, I don't go by a bar or spend time with the boys. I will admit I come in the back door when I get home and I do try to avoid my wife, if at all possible. The reason I don't want to see her is, first of all, because she never has a positive word to say. It's always one big complaint. Secondly, I don't want to see her because usually she looks like a wreck. Her hair is still up in curlers and she is wearing that chenille robe, which she knows I hate. I agree it's a boring life, but I don't know what to do about it.

They both professed their love for one another and stated that they did not want to get a divorce. They were willing to receive counsel, so I set up a plan for them. I started with the wife.

"Here's what I want you to do. As soon as you get home, take your chenille robe and throw it in the trash. When you get up Monday morning [this was a Friday afternoon], I want you to fix yourself up and get the house in order as soon as you can. Then I want you to cook one of your husband's favorite meals. When he drives into the driveway, I want you to go out the front door, meet him on the porch, throw your arms around him and tell him how much you love him."

"That will never work," she protested.

"Try it," I said. Then I proceeded to give the husband his instructions.

"On your way home from work Monday afternoon, I want you to stop by the florist and get your wife a bouquet of flowers. Then when you get home, don't go in the back door. I want you to go in the front door and greet your wife, give her the flowers, take her in your arms and tell her much you love her."

"That will never work, but I will try it if you tell me to," he said.

They both reluctantly agreed to go along with the plan, but they left the office still declaring that it would not work because it was "programmed" behavior, not from the heart. How wrong they were.

When they arrived in my office the next week, they had obviously undergone quite a transformation in their relationship. They came in holding hands and smiling from ear to ear. When I asked how things had gone, each deferred to the other until I finally had to insist on someone taking the lead.

"Well, I thought about it all weekend," the wife began. "We never did discuss it, so I figured he had forgotten it. But on Monday I went ahead with my end of the bargain. I did throw away my old robe. I was surprised; I was glad to see it go. I got myself fixed up and took care of the house. It made me feel good about myself. I even had some time to read and relax. But all day long I couldn't help wondering if my husband had remembered what he was supposed to do."

"Oh, I didn't forget," the husband broke in. "Since she didn't bring up the subject over the weekend, I figured the deal was off. But I was determined to do what I had promised. So I stopped by the florist on the way home and got the flowers. I'll have to admit I started getting more and more excited the closer to home I got."

"Talk about getting excited," she said. "I thought my heart was going to beat out of my chest when I saw his car pulling up in the driveway. But when he got out of the car and I saw that bouquet in his hand, it was more than I could take."

"Was it ever!" he exclaimed. "I hardly got out of the car when she came flying out the front door, ran to me and gave me the biggest, longest hug I've ever had. And she couldn't stop crying. I tell you, it's been like a honeymoon ever since."

I saw that couple several times after that. They continued to maintain that vibrancy in their relationship. They learned to put into practice in their marriage the principle of intentionality. They intentionally loved each other, gave to each other, and listened to each other. Their life of despair and boredom was changed to one of joy and excitement.

All through the Bible, God uses family images to tell His story. As the Father He is loving, in charge, making plans, keeping things in order. As the Son He is the Bridegroom, giving Himself to "per- fect" His bride; going away, but keeping in touch; and coming again in power and glory to catch away His bride. The bride is depicted as waiting, watching, preparing, occupying, keeping herself pure. Marriage is a vivid image: "Let us rejoice and be glad and give him glory! For the wedding of the Lamb has come, and his bride has made herself ready" (Revelation 19:7). The Marriage Supper is a time of great rejoicing, fellowshiping, reminiscing. Living happily ever after in a fantastically beautiful heavenly home is the culmination of this incomparable family love story.

The eternal heavenly home described in the Scriptures gives us an idea of what an earthly home should be like.

Our heavenly home is

- *Beautiful*—walls of jasper, gates of pearl, streets of gold
- *Bright*—glory of God illuminates; Lamb is the light; no night
- *Pure and holy*—nothing enters that would defile.
- *Place of provision*—river of life, fruit of life, fruit every month
- *Happy and joyful*—sounds of rejoicing and praise; no more tears

Our earthly home should be

- *Beautiful*—whether a mansion or a tent, love dwells there.
- *Bright*—light from loving, joyful lives shine brightest at home.
- *Pure and holy*—no unholy influence allowed from television, literature, music, conversation.
- *Place of provision*—every need is met; it is a sanctuary.
- *Happy and joyful*—the strongest, toughest, sweetest love is shown.

Family relationships should be the most joyful of all. Home should be a place of warmth, strength, and protection. It can only be that way if individual family members, beginning with the husband and father, will fulfill their spiritual responsibilities. Unfortunately, this is not always the case. Sometimes it takes only one member, however, acting as salt and light to make the home a brighter, better place.

Joyful in Relationship With Friends

Earlier, the passion of the apostle Paul for his friends was noted. Look again at the Philippian passage where Paul spoke eloquently when he thought about his friends and his experiences in Philippi: "I love you and long to see you, for you are my joy and my reward" (4:1, *TLB*).

Wouldn't it be wonderful if every believer could feel this way about those in the church with whom he or she worked? Is this too idealistic? Were the people at Philippi that much better than the ordinary, run-of-the-mill church members? We know the answers to those questions. Paul wasn't being idealistic nor was he practicing early-church psychology. The church at Philippi had people with problems; Paul simply chose to focus on the positive aspects of his relationship with them, and as he did his heart filled with overflowing joy. This is why he could write with such feeling.

To experience joy in your relationship with friends, you must consciously and arbitrarily think the best about them. Put up with their foibles, their shortcomings and mistakes. Practice the kind of love that doesn't make lists of negative things. This is essentially what Paul was talking about in Philippians 4:8: "Finally, brothers, whatever is true, whatever is noble, whatever is right, whatever is pure, whatever is lovely, whatever is admirable—if anything is excellent or praiseworthy—think about such things." This is not a suggestion; it is a command.

Here is Paul's beautiful formula for his relationship with friends:

- He thought good things, not bad things about them.
- This made his heart overflow with love and joy toward them.
- He let them know how much he thought of them.

The third point is so important. Every time you experience a good feeling about someone, or every time you have a warm thought about someone, let him or her know. Don't keep your good feelings to yourself. Paul put his good feelings down on parchment. It blessed the people at Philippi, and it is still blessing us today. Be joyful in your relationship with your friends. It pays great dividends.

Joyful in Relationship With Foes

Now we come to the most difficult requirement yet. It sounds unreasonable to say that you should be joyful in your relationship with people who are your enemies, who revile you, who persecute you, who criticize you. Does that make sense? No, not from the human perspective. But we're not dealing with the human perspective here. We're talking about divine law. We're talking about a spiritual response to a very practical problem.

"So they departed from the presence of the council, rejoicing that they were counted worthy to suffer shame for His name" (Acts 5:41, NKJV).

"Consider it pure joy, my brothers, whenever you face trials of many kinds" (James 1:2).

In the Sermon on the Mount, Jesus taught that when you are persecuted and opposed, when people say bad things about you, you are to rejoice and be exceedingly glad. It is not a matter of being so superspiritual that nothing hurts or upsets you. It is that you are using a practical spiritual truth that actually neutralizes opposition and criticism through the conscious appropriation of joy.

Understand that this appropriated joy in a negative relationship is not just pulled out of thin air. The primary source of joy in this case flows from our relationship with God. Again, we return to that basic premise of loving God first. Opposition from others is filtered through the fabric of our bond with the Lord. That dynamic gave the disciples the ability to actually rejoice in suffering. They knew that nothing could separate them from the love of God (Romans 8:35-39). We may face opposition, trouble, trial, or even death; but we are never separated from the love of God which is in Christ Jesus.

A side benefit of rejoicing in persecution and suffering is the strong impact it has on the perpetrators of the opposition. When Paul and Silas were severely beaten in Philippi and thrown in the innermost prison, at the midnight hour they sang and rejoiced. This made such an impression on the jailer that when the earthquake set Paul and Silas free, the jailer was ready to repent and be baptized along with his entire household (see Acts 16:22-34). One of the surest ways to make friends out of foes is to handle their opposition with joy. Probably one of the dear friends Paul referred to in his letter as his "joy and reward" was none other than this same Philippian jailer.

God wants joy to be at the heart of every relationship, whether with family, friends, or foes.

CHAPTER 9

The Law of Fruitbearing

Most of my early years were spent in the central valley of California around Fresno. This beautiful part of America is called the "Fruit Basket of the Nation." I learned a lot about fruit while living there. I picked a lot of fruit—peaches, apricots, nectarines, plums, grapes. I ate a lot of fruit. I grew and pruned and nurtured a lot of fruit trees and grape vines.

Fruit is a wonderful creation of God. The trees and vines that produce fruit are beautiful in themselves, especially when they are covered with blossoms or laden with ripening fruit. Mature, fully ripe fruit looks good, smells good, even feels good. And, most pleasing of all, it tastes wonderful! However, the most important thing about fruit is that it is good for you. In fact, it is absolutely essential to proper nutrition and a balanced diet.

The Bible has much to say about fruit. It is almost always spoken of in positive terms. It is used often as a symbol, as a metaphor. In the Garden of Eden, it was depicted as representing knowledge, and its beauty was used by the serpent to tempt Eve: "When the woman saw that the fruit of the tree was good for food and pleasing to the eye, and also desirable for gaining wisdom, she took some and ate it" (Genesis 3:6). Fruit symbolizes the blessings of God: "He will love you and bless you and multiply you; He will also bless the fruit of your womb and the fruit of your land" (Deuteronomy 7:13, *NKJV*). Sometimes, the symbol of fruit represents negative or evil things: "The labour of the righteous tendeth to life; the fruit of the wicked to sin" (Proverbs 10:16, KJV); "Make a tree bad and its fruit will be bad, for a tree is recognized by its fruit" (Matthew 12:33).

For the most part, especially in the New Testament, fruit represents human behavior. Jesus talked about good trees and bad trees, good fruit and bad fruit. Probably the best- known passage in the Bible dealing with good fruit is found in the Book of Galatians:

But the fruit of the Spirit is love, joy, peace, patience, kindness, goodness, faithfulness, gentleness and self-control. Against such things there is no law (5:22, 23).

The negative side of human behavior, the bad fruit, is referred to as "the works of the flesh" or "the acts of the sinful nature":

The acts of the sinful nature are obvious: sexual immorality, impurity and debauchery; idolatry and witchcraft; hatred, discord, jealousy, fits of rage, selfish ambition, dissensions, factions and envy; drunkenness, orgies, and the like. I warn you, as I did before, that those who live like this will not inherit the kingdom of God (5:19-21).

So in the Scriptural sense, *fruit* is defined as "the character of our behavior toward others." That behavior includes both the verbal and nonverbal. It is also essential to understand that no behavior is totally personal and private. Every act on our part, good or bad, public or private, affects our relationships with other people (Romans 14:7). In that sense, then, the quality of our relationships is determined by the fruit we bear.

The Law of Production

Every person bears some kind of spiritual fruit. "He is like a tree planted by streams of water, which yields its fruit in season" (Psalm 1:3). In the Bible, human beings are often characterized as trees, branches, vines, or plants, indicating that they are producers of some kind of fruit. As it is the nature of a tree to produce some kind of natural fruit, so it is the nature of human beings to produce some kind of spiritual fruit.

It follows, then, that the spiritual fruit will be either good or bad. It will be either nourishing or unhealthful. Our behavior will either make people feel better or make them feel worse. "Likewise every good tree bears good fruit, but a bad tree bears bad fruit. A good tree cannot bear bad fruit, and a bad tree cannot bear good fruit" (Matthew 7:17, 18).

Jesus said we will be identified and judged by the kind of fruit we produce—by the kind of behavior we exhibit: "Thus, by their fruit you will recognize them" (Matthew 7:20); "A tree is recognized by its fruit" (12:33).

The Bible clearly identifies what is good fruit and what is bad fruit. A number of scriptures refer to negative, sinful behavior— the kind of behavior that makes people physically, mentally, and spiritually sick. This is *bad* fruit. Here is an even more extensive list, taken right from the Bible: sexual immorality (adultery, fornication, homosexuality, and other sexual perversions), impurity of mind, sensuality, idolatry, witchcraft, hatred, discord, jealousy, fits of rage, selfish ambitions, dissensions, factions, envy, drunkenness, and orgies (Galatians 5:19-21; Romans 13:13; 1 Corinthians 6:8, 9; 1 Timothy 1:9, 10).

Some people use the excuse "It's not in the Bible" in order to legitimize sinful behavior. There is no exhaustive list of sins, not even in the Bible. The devil is very creative in producing new varieties and strains of bad fruit on a regular basis. Suffice it to say that if it looks bad, smells bad, tastes bad, and it makes you sick, it is bad. Don't touch it, handle it, or take a bite of it.

While there is a list of bad fruit in the Scriptures, there is also a list of good fruit. Notice these positive behaviors: love, joy, peace, patience, kindness, goodness, faithfulness, gentleness, self-control, humility, compassion, deference, preference, forbearance, courtesy, hospitality, sensitivity, understanding, and appreciation (Galatians 5:22, 23; Ephesians 4:32; Colossians 3:12, 13). Again, this is not a complete list. Good behavior can always be identified by its healthful, helpful, happy effect upon others.

Your fruit is your behavior. You can tell a tree by its fruit. You can tell a Christian by his behavior.

The Law of Consumption

Jesus did a lot of interesting things, but He never did anything without a purpose. He was always teaching a spiritual truth by what He said and did. Such was the case in His encounter with the fig tree:

> Early in the morning, as he was on his way back to the city, he was hungry. Seeing a fig tree by the road, he went up to

it but found nothing on it except leaves. Then he said to it, "May you never bear fruit again!" Immediately the tree withered (Matthew 21:18, 19).

It is apparent that Jesus expected to find figs on the tree. He was hungry and He anticipated being satisfied by the fruit from the tree. When He found none, He cursed the tree. The point Jesus was making is that trees are supposed to bear fruit and the purpose of that fruit is to be consumed. The ultimate purpose of fruit is reproduction, as we shall see later. However, the consumption of the fruit is a priority. Fruit is made to be consumed—not by the tree, but by someone else.

Whether we like it or not, whether we intend it or not, others will consume the fruit we bear. Our behavior, good or bad, will affect and impact other people. Those we come in contact with, even on a casual basis, are always picking fruit off our branches. There is essentially no "private" behavior. It is a fallacy to think that our behavior, in any given situation, affects only ourselves. Somewhere, somehow, sometime, someone is partaking of that fruit. And the closer the relationship, the greater the impact and influence. This is why our behavior within the confines of our own home is so important. Our spouse and our children are constantly consuming our fruit and are being affected positively or negatively by the experience.

Understand that while the law of consumption is a serious matter, it is also the source of some of our most joyful moments. Since the purpose of a tree is to bear fruit and the purpose of the fruit is to be consumed, we could say that the tree's greatest fulfillment is when this happens. A good tree loves to have its fruit consumed. This is the purpose of its life. This is what it lives for.

My experience with fruit trees has caused me to imagine what it must be like to be, say, a peach tree. It is not easy being a peach tree. At the close of each growing season, in early fall, its green leaves begin to turn yellow and brown. Eventually every one of them drops off. In this stripped, naked condition, the tree faces the bleak, cold winter. But before the onslaught of winter, there must come the "pruning" experience. Most of the growth the tree struggled to put on during the growing season is now unmercifully lopped off. Not only does it lose all its leaves, but also most of its new branches.

Seeing a peach tree in the field during the winter, one could easily assume that it has no life left in it. It looks totally dead. Perhaps the tree feels that way. But it valiantly holds on to life and patiently waits for the first warm rays of the spring sun. When spring does finally arrive, the tree feels its sap begin to flow and senses the formation of tiny green buds at the tips of its branches. As warm spring days rush by, some of those tiny green buds unfold into bushels of lush new leaves, while others burst forth into cascades of fragrant pink or white flowers. Soon the leaves mature and the flowers fade. In place of the flowers, there develops a tiny nub that quickly forms a small peach.

Now the fruit is the focus of all the tree's efforts.

As spring turns to summer, the culmination of all this work is at hand. A beautiful, fragrantly ripe peach hangs at the end of one of the branches. But this is not yet the fulfillment of the peach tree's dream.

The moment finally arrives. A young man enters the orchard. "Where is that wonderful aroma coming from? Could it be there is already a ripe peach this early in the season?" Following his nose, he comes to the tree and spies the luscious, plump peach. He eagerly plucks it from the branch, gently rubs away the surface fuzz, and deliberately takes a huge, satisfying bite. The warm, sweet juice drips off the end of his chin. He wipes his mouth with the sleeve of his shirt. "Man," he says, "that's the best peach I've ever tasted in all my life!"

Now the peach tree is fulfilled. Its dreams are realized. All the struggle, the traumatic "pruning," the hard work, seem as nothing. It flutters its leaves in exultation and exclaims, "This is the reason I was born!"

We can find no greater joy, no more wonderful fulfillment than to know that our good fruit has added strength and happiness to another's life. After Jesus ministered to the woman at the well (John 4), He refused to eat, telling His disciples that He had food they knew not of. His spirit was feasting on the experience of seeing a broken, sinful woman transformed into a living witness of the delivering power of God.

This kind of joy is at the heart of what this book is about. This is how God intended relationships to be—satisfying and fulfilling. It is not easy to bear the fruit of the Spirit in a consistent way. Some relationships can be difficult. We have to really work at them. But, in the end, the rewards far outweigh the sacrifices.

To have someone who is hungry or hurting come under our branches and receive nourishment and healing brings a sense of spiritual fulfillment that cannot be put into words.

An important point to remember with regard to the law of consumption is that the character of the fruit (its goodness or bad-ness) is determined only by the tasting. "The proof of the pudding is in the eating." Our behavior is ultimately judged by the effect it has on other people. Does it make them healthier and happier, or does it make them sicker and more depressed?

You can't always judge fruit by the way it looks. These days the manufacture of artificial fruit has been perfected. Sometimes it is difficult to distinguish this man-made item from the real thing. They even add fuzz to artificial peaches.

Some people go to a store and purchase real-looking artificial fruit to hang on their branches. They are not willing to make the commitment to live for God and to be plugged into the True Vine. Their fruit looks real from a distance and in some cases even up close. There is only one sure way to tell the difference. Take a bite. When you are expecting a bite of sweet, nourishing good fruit and wind up with a mouthful of wax or plastic, you are extremely dis-appointed and you may get sick. This is what happens when we run into deceptive, hypocritical behavior from others.

And we need to remember that others feel this way when we are guilty of that kind of behavior ourselves.

How is your behavior affecting the people around you, espe-cially those closest to you? Are they stronger or weaker because of the way you live? This is an important question, because the way it is answered determines not only a sense of happiness and ful-fillment here, but also one's place in eternity.

The Law of Reproduction

The apostle Paul understood the law of reproduction when he wrote to the believers in Rome:

Now I do not want you to be unaware, brethren, that I often planned to come to you (but was hindered until now), that I might have some fruit among you also, just as among the other Gentiles (Romans 1:13, *NKJV*).

The law of reproduction refers to one of God's immutable truths: "Each produces after its own kind." Fruit reproduces fruit. Good fruit reproduces good fruit. Bad fruit reproduces bad fruit. This concept is closely related to another of God's basic laws: "You will reap what you sow." Whatever kind of fruit you give out (what you sow) is the kind you will receive in turn.

Within every fruit is a seed that gives it the potential to reproduce itself. Within every behavior is the power for that behavior to repeat itself in the person being impacted. In this case, we usually consume the seeds. On the other hand, we sometimes learn how to spit them out so they won't grow in us. For the most part, seeds are consumed and they start to grow and produce a like kind of fruit. This law of reproduction leads to the basic problems in society today.

Through the centuries, society has tried various ways to get rid of bad fruit. It has been tried through the enactment of laws, the building of jails, the establishment of clinics, and the development of educational programs. Some believe that the only way to destroy bad fruit is to kill the producer. All of these methods continue today. But these methods of improving human behavior have never worked, and never will, because the true source of bad fruit is not being addressed.

Jesus taught that the only way to stop the bearing of bad fruit is to change the character of the tree. He talked about being "born again." He said it is possible to be grafted into a new tree, a good tree, a tree of righteousness. The old stock is sinful and produces only bad fruit; but the new stock (Jesus Christ) will produce only good fruit.

We must understand the powerful impact of our behavior (fruit) on others. Good fruit not only makes people feel better for the moment, but the seed that is consumed will begin to grow and will produce more of that same good fruit over the course of a lifetime.

When our children were growing up, I tried to make it a habit to help my wife by clearing the table after every meal. My two sons generally always helped me with this chore. They are both now married with families of their own, but one of my continuing sources of satisfaction is to see those two sons repeating that same good behavior in their own homes. A small thing perhaps, but it keeps generating profitable returns—a satisfaction to their dad, a blessing to their wives, and a great example to their children.

Unfortunately, what is true for good behavior is also true for bad behavior. According to Deuteronomy 5, the sins of the father have repercussions on the children to the third and fourth generations. Alcoholism tends to produce alcoholism. Abuse produces abuse. The only way this vicious cycle can be broken is for an intervention of the delivering power of God. That intervention comes through the life of an individual who has made a commitment to God and is thereby empowered to bear good fruit which ultimately will break the cycle.

We should be constantly challenged to examine our behavior for its positive or negative impact on others. To close this chapter on the law of fruitbearing, here is a checklist of behavioral traits.

Death in the Bad Fruit

• *Bitter Fruit* - Bad attitudes, harsh criticism, mean spirit, devious behavior, broken confidences

• *Rotten Fruit* - Immoral behavior, sexual sins, dirty mind, shady stories, self-centeredness

• *Green (Unripe) Fruit* - Immature attitudes, pouting, jealousy, envy, strife, fits of rage, profanity

Life in the Good Fruit

• *Sweet Fruit* - Tenderness, courtesy, kindness, compassion, gentleness love that is sincere and without hypocrisy

• *Fresh Fruit* - Purity, integrity, genuineness, goodness, faithfulness, love that is centered on others

• *Ripe Fruit* - Joy, peace, patience, deference, preference, forbearance, self-control, love that is "tough"

CHAPTER 10

The Healing of Relationships

H e was one of 12 sons. Next to the youngest. The favorite of his father. The envy of his brothers. His name was Joseph.

Of all the real-life stories in the Bible, Joseph's is one of the most instructive, especially when it comes to human relationships. He had problems with his relationships early in life. For no apparent reason other than sibling rivalry and jealousy, his older brothers hated him. That hatred reached a climax when Joseph was a teenager. So intense was their anger that they planned to kill him, but they compromised and sold him into slavery instead. Not only was Joseph alienated from his brothers, but now he was separated, perhaps forever, from his loving father and the rest of the family. His future did not look promising.

It is important to note that despite this devastating experience that radically affected his life, there is no indication that Joseph ever harbored bitterness toward his brothers. He was deeply hurt, but he did not have a vengeful spirit.

127

Joseph's relationship problems were not over. First, he was hated for no good reason. Then he was accused of a crime he did not commit. His positive attitude and hard work earned him, although a slave, a position as overseer of his master's household. But because Joseph resisted the advances of his master's wife, he was falsely accused by her of sexual harassment and was thrown into prison—again the innocent victim of another person's anger.

Even in prison Joseph's good attitude and obvious intelligence brought him positive recognition. But the people he befriended in prison forgot him once they were released. So again, Joseph experienced the pain of relationships gone wrong.

Jealousy, hatred, anger, separation, false accusations, broken promises—Joseph was hit by them all. But through every one of these negative circumstances, he maintained his integrity and kept himself from a bitter attitude. He did not use the sins and failures of others as an excuse to violate the laws of God in his own behavior. Nor did he allow what had happened to him in the past to keep him from fulfilling the will of God and enjoying the blessings of God in the future.

Joseph's life could have been a disaster. He could have become a bitter, vengeful man. He could have spent his life angry because of what people had done to him. But that is not what happened. His life wound up in a blaze of glory and victory. He was spectacularly successful. He was reconciled to his brothers and reunited with his family. He was happy and fulfilled. What made the difference?

The secret to Joseph's success in his life and relationships is found in the words of his father, Jacob, as recorded in the Book of Genesis. On his deathbed, Jacob called all of his sons before him to say a final word to them. What he said about Joseph is very revealing:

> Joseph is a fruitful vine, a fruitful vine near a spring, whose branches climb over a wall. With bitterness archers attacked him; they shot at him with hostility. But his bow remained steady, his strong arms stayed limber, because of the hand of the Mighty One of Jacob. . . . Your father's blessings are greater than the blessings of the ancient mountains, than the bounty of the age-old hills. Let all these rest on the head of Joseph, on the brow of the prince among his brothers (Genesis 49:22–24, 26).

Joseph had to live with walls in his life—walls of hatred, jealousy, and anger; walls created by other people. How he dealt with those walls, those broken relationships, made the difference between success and failure and between happiness and regret. His solution to walls in his life was to become a fruitful tree and to run his fruitful branch over the wall. What a powerful illustration! Instead of cursing the walls, trying to tear them down, get around them or over them, he just let the fruit of his godly life—love, joy, peace, patience, gentleness, among other traits—reach over the wall and change the people on the other side for the better. Eventually those changed people tore down the walls they had built. This is God's plan for the healing of broken relationships.

The Reality of Broken Relationships

A few years ago I had the honor of being elected to one of the highest councils of my denomination. My picture came out in one of the church publications a few weeks later. It was a privilege to be listed with some of the respected leaders of the church. My family told me they were proud of me. However, the nice feeling did not last long.

Someone tore out a page of that publication and sent it to me through the mail. It was the page with my picture on it. The person had taken artistic license with my photograph and added a moustache, beard . . . and horns. In the white space around the edge of the page were written some choice comments about my character and some accusations that were totally untrue.

Of course there was no signature and no way to trace the origin of the letter.

My feelings went from being hurt to being curious to being angry. I wanted to find out who would do such a thing. I tried to analyze the handwriting. I wracked my brain trying to come up with a clue from recent relationship situations. Nothing. Finally, I decided it wasn't worth any more time. I prayed about it and left it with the Lord. I knew there was probably nothing I could do to change the person's mind anyway. Still, it was frustrating to think that someone could form those opinions and I didn't even know who that person was, let alone having the opportunity to refute those opinions.

Several months went by and I had not thought much more about my "devil" picture. Then one evening at the close of a church service where I was ministering, a man approached me and with tears disclosed that he was the one who had sent the letter. He said he felt badly about the letter to begin with, but that his guilt had been greatly multiplied because, in the meantime, I had been so nice to him and had even gone out of my way to help him in a certain situation. Despite the embarrassment, he said, he had to make the matter right.

On his own he decided to tear down the wall he had built. Needless to say, I experienced a lot of joy and relief that evening and every time I thought about it after that. It stills makes me feel good today. The only little qualm I have is wondering whether or not I would have treated the man so well had I known he was my secret enemy. Hopefully, I would have.

We cannot control the attitudes and actions of other people toward us. Some people, even so-called friends, will build walls of resentment and misunderstanding and we are helpless to stop them. The only control we have in circumstances like that is to control our response to those walls.

People build walls for many reasons.

Differences. One of the chief reasons people build walls is because of differences. That was a major factor in the difficulties between Joseph and his brothers. Joseph had a different mother. He was younger. He was a dreamer and not a sheepherder. He was the favorite of his father. All of us are different, and those differences can lead to disagreements and ultimately to broken relationships if we are not careful. But as careful as we are, sometimes those differences lead to the building of relationship walls.

Differences can be caused by background, culture, race, sex, age, and just basic personality types. Husbands and wives generally have many built-in differences which they bring into a marriage. Those differences can create walls that are extremely detrimental to marital happiness. Even mundane things like the time to get up or the time to go to bed can cause big problems. Perhaps she has been used to turning in early so she can get her "beauty sleep." He is in the habit of watching the late, late show. When he finally falls into bed at 1 a.m. and maybe feeling a little amorous, he may discover quickly that a wall has already begun to be built. Reaching over the walls of differences with the fruit of understanding and acceptance will solve a lot of problems.

Deceit. Another cause for the building of walls is deceit. In Joseph's case, his master's wife told a lie on him and in a moment everything changed. What had been a pleasant, positive relationship now became adversarial and confrontational. A wall was built because of an untruth and Joseph was put in prison, alienated from his master's family. Deceit will destroy a relationship. That is why God hates "a lying tongue" and "a false witness who pours out lies" (Proverbs 6:17, 19). While we cannot keep others from telling untruths, we must be certain that we are always truthful in our relationships. "Do not lie to each other, since you have taken off your old self with its practices" (Colossians 3:9).

There really is no sure way to defend ourselves against lies. There are sometimes circumstances in which it is possible to directly confront someone who has told an untruth. However, that is a rare situation and does not always bring profitable results. Generally, we have to practice forbearance and take it on the chin. We have to reach over the wall of deceit with a fruitful bough laden with integrity, faithfulness, goodness, and self-control. That's what Joseph did. It worked for him. It will also work for us because it is the law of God.

Defensiveness. This also creates walls in relationships. Even though they were older, Joseph's brothers were jealous of him. In some ways they felt inferior to him. He was his father's favorite. Jacob had given him a coat of many colors, which probably signified special honor and authority. He had dreams which they didn't like or understand. Also Joseph had brought negative reports to their father about the conduct of his brothers. All these things did not make for a positive relationship between Joseph and his brothers.

Many relationship problems stem from a defensive attitude on the part of one or both parties. This "psychological touchiness" permeates all aspects of behavior. When a person does not feel good about himself, it is difficult for him to relate positively to others. A poor self-image will make one vulnerable to a number of attitudes that militate against good relationships. A lack of self-confidence opens the door for jealousy, envy, hatred, bitterness, and strife.

It is important to understand the spiritual dimension of defensiveness. The devil knows too well the negative spiritual implications of a defensive attitude. That is why he works so hard to put us down, to accuse us, and to intimidate us. He is aware that when we are "down" on ourselves, we have a difficult time being "up" on anyone else. On the other hand, as we shall see later, when our confidence level is strong, we see others with a more balanced perspective. We can handle the many variables of relationship so much better.

When someone in your life builds a wall because of a defensive attitude, keep in mind that you are probably not to blame. You may simply be the most accessible person at the moment upon whom some frustration can be vented. Run your fruitful branch over the wall and bless that person with some love, forgiveness, and acceptance.

The Pattern for Restored Relationships

Joseph's story has a happy ending. A happy ending was, and is, God's idea. He intends for every story to end this way. He has the greatest happy ending imaginable planned for His Son and His Son's bride, the church.

When we all get to heaven, what a day of rejoicing that will be! When we all see Jesus, we'll sing and shout the victory.

That will be the culmination of the joy of our relationship with the Lord. But God wants earthly relationships also to be joyful.

In Joseph's case, he was reconciled to his brothers and he was reunited with his father. It was an overwhelmingly joyful experience for him. The Bible says: "Then Joseph could not restrain himself before all those who stood by him. . . . And he wept aloud, and the Egyptians and the house of Pharaoh heard it. . . . So Joseph made ready his chariot and went up to Goshen to meet his father Israel; and he presented himself to him, and fell on his neck and wept on his neck a good while (Genesis 45:1, 2; 46:29, *NKJV*).

There is no greater joy than the joy of reconciliation and restoration. When the Prodigal Son returned home, his father ran to meet him and enfolded his son with a joyful embrace. Jesus also talked about the joy in heaven when a son is reconciled: "There is rejoicing in the presence of the angels of God over one sinner who repents" (Luke 15:10). The sadness and grief of separation is turned into the joy of restoration.

The pattern that Joseph followed to bring about the restoration of his family is instructive for us today. This pattern worked because it was based on his relationship with Jehovah God. The way Joseph lived his life and the way he responded to the walls built by his brothers and other people give us insight into how to deal with our own broken relationships.

Joseph healed broken relationships because he demonstrated

personal *integrity*. His father, Jacob, described it this way: "His bow remained steady [strong]" (Genesis 49:24). He never wavered in his commitment to do the right thing. He was consistent in his example. He was honest and truthful in all of his dealings. That stability and dependability finally paid off, as it always will.

When other people build walls and shut us out of their lives, the greatest asset we have is our own spiritual strength which flows from our relationship with God. That again is why the order of the Great Commandment is so important. Before we can properly relate to others, we must first love God with all our heart, soul, mind, and strength. Joseph knew God was with him despite the circumstances he found himself in at any particular time. Whether in the pit or in prison, he had confidence that God would deliver him. His spiritual strength gave him favor with other people and provided the basis for reconciliation with those from whom he was separated.

Joseph saw the pattern of events in his life, even negative things, as God's doing. Thus he was able to cope with his brothers' selling him into slavery without feeling resentful and taking vengeance when he could. Looking at their evil deeds as he did made it easier for him to forgive them. Here is how he explained it to his brothers:

But now, do not . . . be grieved or angry with yourselves because you sold me here; for God sent me before you to preserve life. . . . And God sent me before you to preserve a posterity for you in the earth, and to save your lives by a great deliverance. So now it was not you who sent me here, but God (Genesis 45:5, 7, 8, *NKJV*).

When we understand that God is sovereign in our lives, we will not be so quick to blame others for the bad things that happen to us. When we don't blame others, we feel no need for revenge or retribution. That kind of attitude leaves the door open for others to admit their wrongs and to give and receive forgiveness.

Joseph healed broken relationships because he demonstrated spiritual insight. This quality helped bring family together again. Integrity and spiritual insight go hand in hand. Joseph understood what was going on with his brothers. He was spiritually sensitive. He was easily touched. He wept with his brothers and with his father. Jesus portrayed this aspect of human relationships so beautifully. Many times the Gospels speak of Jesus being "moved with compassion." When He saw the multitudes, He knew what was going on with them. He sensed the spiritual hunger of the woman at the well.

Without this kind of spiritual insight and sensitivity, it is doubtful there can be any real healing of broken relationships. It is a lack of this relational attention that is the cause of so much alienation and misunderstanding between husbands and wives, parents and children.

When I was doing an internship at a psychiatric hospital during my doctoral studies, I saw one of the most shocking examples of insensitivity imaginable. I was asked to counsel a young lady who was in custody for attempting to kill her father. She told me how her father, a high-ranking military officer, never paid any attention to her. He would come home from work at night, and even though she was in the room he passed through, he would hardly ever acknowledge her. Sometimes she would get in his face and say, "Look at me. I'm your daughter." But he would push her aside and go on reading his paper. Such conduct by a father is hard to believe, but it was verified by other family members.

The girl finally began to act out in other, more serious, ways. She wrecked the family car. She had an affair with an older man. Still her father refused to get involved in her life. Finally, in desperation one night, she tried to stab her father with a butcher knife. In our first counseling sessions, she emphatically stated how much she hated her father. "When he dies, I will dance on his grave," she said. Then one day, she started to cry. "I don't hate my father." Now she was heaving with sobs. "I don't hate him; I love him. I just want him to pay attention to me." To my knowledge, that father never was able to properly respond to the cry of his daughter.

Relationships will be healed when we learn to "weep with those who weep" and "rejoice with those who rejoice" (Romans 12:15). Joseph knew how to do that.

Finally, Joseph healed broken relationships and was reconciled with his family because he took the *initiative*. Integrity, insight, initiative—this is the pattern Joseph used. And what a beautiful result he achieved. He didn't wait for his brothers to seek reconciliation, he offered it. He didn't ask for an apology, he told them one wasn't necessary. He anticipated their questions and consoled their fears. He was a peacemaker. His fruitful bough ran over that wall of hatred and bitterness and caused it to crumble to dust.

How about you? Do you have any walls in your life right now? Reevaluate the way you have been handling those troubled relationships. Maybe the Lord wants you to stop what you have been

doing and sink your roots deeper into His Word and let your fruitful branch reach over that wall. You might be surprised how the
folks on the other side respond.

PART 3

Loving Ourselves

* * *

*For God did not give us
a spirit of timidity,
but a spirit of power,
of love and of self-discipline.*

2 Timothy 1:7

CHAPTER 11

The Apple of His Eye

A t the outset of this section on "loving ourselves," it is important to stress again the order God gives to relationship: God, others, self. The understanding of and respect for that order is absolutely essential before we move on. God's priorities must be followed if we expect His blessings. Always, in every way, we must love God first and most. Everything that happens in our lives must be processed first through that primary relationship. Flowing out of a right relationship with God is a love for others. We cannot love God without loving others, and we cannot love others without loving God.

Having emphasized these two vital steps, it is essential now to take the third step. We must complete the cycle God created. We must talk about loving ourself. However, this subject has to be approached carefully and Scripturally because it involves a lot of misunderstanding and misinformation.

One of the biggest problems is that secular humanism has

inverted God's order and placed love of self first on the list. This idea has been at the forefront of the humanist agenda for the past 30 years. It has greatly impacted popular psychology and has even infected some aspects of Christian theology. Coupled with this overemphasis on self by the secular world is an equally erroneous de-emphasis in certain areas of the church world. Some religious teachers would have us kill self or, with others, deny its very existence.

But God always has a beautiful balance. He doesn't want us to exalt self or debase it or deny its existence. He wants self to be acknowledged, respected, and given its proper place. We won't have to worry about sinful self-centeredness or egoism if we follow God's order and practice God's balance. Oswald Chambers, author of the classic *My Utmost for His Highest*, states in his book *Biblical Psychology*: "The teaching of our Lord and of the Apostle Paul continually centers around 'I,' yet there is no egotism about it . . . everything in the Bible is related to man, to his salvation, to his sanctification, to his keeping" (p. 152).

The idea of loving oneself did not originate with man. It was designed by God to complete the cycle of love relationships. If we love God, that, in turn, helps us to sincerely love others. When our relationship with God and with others is on track, we will feel good about our- self. And when we love and respect ourself, it will not be difficult to love others and to give God His supreme place in our life. It was God who made this third step an integral part of the Great Commandment. If we try to ignore it or change it, we violate the Word of God and that can have dire consequences.

It makes sense that God would want our self-esteem to be high. I know how I feel about my own two sons and daughter. I don't want any of them to struggle with a negative self-image. I know how devastating and debilitating such a feeling can be. If that should happen, as a caring father I would do whatever I could to build them up and to help them feel better about themselves. On the other hand, if one of those children became arrogant and self-centered, I would have to take the responsibility to let that child know the error of his or her ways. That is the way God views His relationship with us. He wants our view of ourself to be balanced.

The Problem With Feelings of Inferiority

Reality is that most people don't have an overly high view of themselves and their abilities. Just the opposite is true. Most people, in their "heart of hearts," don't feel good about themselves. They worry about their physical appearance. They question the success of their role as a spouse, parent, child, or friend. They wonder about their relationship with God.

The results of a simple survey give credence to the idea of a widespread problem with feelings of inferiority. In an experiment that has been conducted in several different ways with groups and individuals over the years, people are asked to list 10 things about themselves that they don't like. The time it takes to complete this exercise is noted. Then, they are asked to list 10 things about themselves they like. A strange thing happens. It takes much longer to finish the "positive" list than it does to complete the "negative" one. In fact, most people never finish the second list. The survey is always anonymous and generally is not seen by anyone else. The point is not the list, but the fact that people find it relatively easy to think of negative things about themselves while struggling to think of positive things.

Self-image is a problem, often, for good reasons. Many people grow up today in an environment that is not conducive to building self-esteem. When there is divorce, abuse, or neglect, the tendency is for those involved, whether the perpetrators or not, to develop a sense of guilt and blame themselves. Sometimes, unrealistic expectations set by parents and others undermine self-confidence. The false images portrayed by Hollywood and approved by society can devastate those who feel they don't measure up. However, the greatest reason for the erosion of self-esteem and the feelings of inferiority is the accusatory message sent by the devil. Every day in dozens of different ways, he is putting us down. He is constantly whispering negative things in our ear. He tests us, taunts us, and tempts us. Unless we understand how to spiritually resist him, his persistent message will shape how we feel about ourselves.

The paradoxical aspect of this situation is that a poor self-image generally leads to behavior that is self-centered and socially unacceptable: drugs, promiscuity, vandalism, gang activity, white-collar crime, and a general disregard for the rights of others; arrogance, jealousy, insolence, hatred, and bitterness. These are just a few examples of behavior caused by negative feelings about oneself. While some turn outward in displaying their frustrations, others turn inward and retreat into a dark world of their own. The great contradiction is that behavior that appears to be selfish and attitudes that are assumed to be egotistical are really generated from feelings of inferiority. The devil knows this fact well, and that is why he is increasing his attacks and escalating his accusations.

But God holds the solution to this dilemma. He wants a close relationship with us—like a father with a son. He offers His love to strengthen and sustain us. He promises His blessings and pro-

144

tection. He gives us power over all our enemies. He calls to us as He did to Joshua: "Yes, be bold and strong! Banish fear and doubt! For remember, the Lord your God is with you wherever you go" (Joshua 1:9, *TLB*). God really does love us and He wants us to feel good about ourself.

God's Joy in Us

In Moses' farewell address to the children of Israel, he repeated the words of God to His people: "For the Lord's portion is his people, Jacob his allotted inheritance. In a desert land he found him, in a barren and howling waste. He shielded him and cared for him; he guarded him as the apple of his eye" (Deuteronomy 32:9, 10).

The expression "the apple of his eye" has come to denote something special, something precious, something regarded as a favorite. It refers to the eyeball itself, which is treasured and thus protected and covered. This way God described His feelings for His people—precious, treasured, a favorite. The children of Israel could not doubt how Jehovah felt about them. He had delivered them out of Egypt. He had clothed them, fed them, and protected them in the wilderness. Now He was about to give them Canaan as their inheritance. He had proved His love over and over. That made Israel feel special . . . and they were.

Those tender words are relevant for God's children today. He calls you the apple of His eye because of His love for you. The expression makes me think of my daughter-in-law, Kim. When she and Bob moved into a new house, she talked about the joy she was getting from her new kitchen. The thing she liked best about the kitchen was not the cupboards or the appliances, but the window over the sink where she could watch her children at play. That's how it is with God and His children. He gets joy out of simply watching over them.

A rarely quoted scripture from a little-known minor prophet gives a vivid description of God's feelings for His people: "The Lord your God is with you he is mighty to save. He will take great delight in you, he will quiet you with his love, he will rejoice over you with singing" (Zephaniah 3:17).

It is difficult for me to imagine God rejoicing and singing, but that is what the prophet says. In fact, the Hebrew meaning is even stronger. The word *rejoice* actually means to "whirl around." Picture that! On the other hand, as God watches over us, He recognizes we sometimes get into difficult situations. So He promises His presence to save and His love to bring a calmness. As His people, could we ask for any more wonderful testimony of His nearness to us?

Of all the happy events in life, nothing brings greater joy than a wedding. And the two happiest people there are the bride and the bridegroom. God uses the beautiful companionship between the new husband and wife to illustrate the bond He shares with His people. "As a bridegroom rejoices over his bride, so will your God rejoice over you" (Isaiah 62:5). The Song of Solomon goes into exquisite detail describing the wondrous relationship between the beloved and the lover.

One of the sure signs of true love is the pleasure of being in one another's company. Just being together is enough. There doesn't have to be an agenda, nothing special to do, not even words are necessary. God likes to be around His people. "The Lord takes delight in his people" (Psalm 149:4). He calls them His vineyard, a garden in which He takes great delight (Isaiah 5:7). He delights, or rejoices, in their well-being (Psalm 35:27).

What is the purpose of God seemingly going out of His way to express His joy in us? Does God need this kind of relationship? Obviously, this is not for God's benefit but for ours. He wants us to know how valuable we are to Him. We need to believe that God means what He says when He tells us how much He loves us. If we confidently believe that and understand its implications, it will do a lot to strengthen our self-image. As the "apple of his eye," we enjoy a special place in His heart.

God's Concern for Us

God's love for us and His joy in us extends to us in a very practical way. He pays attention to what is going on with us. He is concerned about what happens to us. Because He cares, He wants us to relax in our relationship with Him and let Him be responsible for the weightier issues in our life. Eugene Peterson's recently published translation of the New Testament, called *The Message*, gives a fresh and authentic voice to the Scriptures. Here is his rendering of Luke 12:25-28:

> Has anyone by fussing before the mirror ever gotten taller by so much as an inch? If fussing can't even do that, why fuss at all? Walk into the fields and look at the wildflowers. They don't fuss with their appearance—but have you ever seen color and design quite like it? The ten best-dressed men and women in the country look shabby alongside them. If God gives such attention to the wildflowers, most of them never even seen, don't you think he'll attend to you, take pride in you, do his best for you?

Again, God is telling us not to fuss and worry over things we can't do anything about. He reinforces that admonition by showing us how He cares for the birds of the air and the flowers of the field and then telling us how much more important we are than those. He cares for us not just because we are human beings but because He values us on a personal basis. Love, to be loved, always has to be personalized. God doesn't deal with us in groups, but as individuals.

A friend of mine had an experience recently that demonstrated God's personal concern for him. Driving home on a busy interstate highway late one afternoon, he was tired and became drowsy. Before he realized it, he had fallen asleep at the wheel while traveling at a high rate of speed. Suddenly he was startled awake by the sound of a small rock hitting his windshield. When he looked up he was shocked to see that he was only a few feet from smashing into the rear of a slow-moving 18-wheeler. With a quick, sharp turn of the steering wheel, he was able to miss the truck by inches. As he regained his composure, he sensed the voice of God speaking in his heart: "I used a little pebble to show My love for you. I still have a work for you to do." That kind of message stays with you forever.

Sometimes God demonstrates His concern for us by His discipline: "My son, do not make light of the Lord's discipline, and do not lose heart when he rebukes you, because the Lord disciplines those he loves, and he punishes everyone he accepts as a son" (Hebrews 12:6). As it is with a loving parent, discipline implies attention. Because God loves us and we are valuable to Him, He will not overlook our disobedience or wink at our sin. He knows what it takes to make us strong, whether in times of rejoicing or repentance.

God's Promise to Us

Over 40 years ago God gave me a promise that He is still in the process of fulfilling. At age 19 I was newly called to preach, struggling in courtship, and (as I mentioned earlier) afflicted with cancer. My self-image was dragging bottom. I had no money and no car. I was a flop as a preacher. I thought I might die physically. Worst of all my hopes for marriage had just been dashed by what I thought was stiff competition from a supposed friend. (Later it turned out he was no competition at all.)

At this low point the Lord gave me Psalm 128:

Blessed is every one that feareth the Lord; that walketh in his ways. For thou shalt eat the labour of thine hands: happy shalt thou be, and it shall be well with thee. Thy wife shall be as a fruitful vine by the sides of thine house: thy children like olive plants round about thy table. Behold, that thus shall the man be blessed that feareth the Lord. The Lord shall bless thee out of Zion: and thou shalt see the good of Jerusalem all the days of thy life. Yea, thou shalt see thy children's children, and peace upon Israel (KJV).

Immediately, my self-esteem went up 200 points. If God was going to do all these things in my life, I would soon be sitting on top of the world. Well, God did keep His word and one by one each promise was fulfilled, all the way through to seeing my children's children—my grandchildren.

A few days ago, I dedicated my sixth grandchild. She was special because she embodied the fulfillment of God's promise, not just to me, but also to my daughter and her husband. After over six years of many petitions and much anxiety, God not only answered the prayers of a dedicated couple, but also fulfilled a promise made many years before to a 19-year-old preacher who was at the end of his rope.

God makes promises to His children and then keeps them because He loves us! His Book is filled with divine commitments that are as good as money in the bank. Don't be anxious. You will have problems and troubles, but He will deliver you out of every one of them. Things may look a little uncertain at times; but don't worry, every step you take will be ordered. Finances may not be flush just when you need them; but count on it, He will supply all of your needs. Your loved ones may be out of the fold; but keep praying, the hounds of heaven are on their trail.

Knowing that God will fulfill every one of His promises that are significant to you should lift your spirits and put joy in your soul. You have no need to find fulfillment from any other source. He is your sufficiency, and you are the apple of His eye.

Believe it!

CHAPTER 12

A
Calm
Assurance

D uring World War II, my family made quite a contribution to the war effort. We were proud of the service flag that hung in our front living room window. Its three blue stars represented my three older brothers who were all serving in the military—one in the Air Force and two in the Navy. Dad supervised a unit in a war-materials depot and later went to Europe as a news photographer.

Since I was too young to serve, I stayed at home with my mother and younger sister to help keep the home fires burning. In a daily ritual Mom led a time of family prayer for the safety of my brothers and my dad. That daily prayer seemed to give Mom peace and the assurance that everything was going to be okay, even when it was weeks between letters from them.

Early one morning around 3 o'clock her calm assurance turned to near panic. Mom shook me out of a sound sleep. She was crying and upset. She said she had the feeling that my brother,

Charles, was in grave danger. After we prayed together for probably 20 minutes, she stopped praying, wiped away her tears and told me she knew Charles was now safe. It was evident that her peace had returned. We took note of the exact time we started praying. Mom was certain we would hear from Charles about a miraculous intervention that could be traced to that precise moment.

Sure enough, a few weeks later the anticipated letter arrived. Charles was stationed on the battleship *Tennessee*, which at that time was engaged in fierce island battles in the South Pacific. As the tide of the war turned against the Japanese, they began to take some desperate measures. One of their tactics was the use of kamikazes, or "suicide planes." A plane would be outfitted with explosives and intentionally crashed into a ship. During the closing days of the war, a number of American ships were sunk by kamikazes.

In his letter Charles related how he and a buddy were on the top deck of the ship when a voice told him to run behind the bulkhead. Suddenly, out of the misty fog came a Japanese kamikaze, slamming into the superstructure of the ship, hitting at almost the same spot my brother had been standing. His buddy was killed and Charles was wounded near his eye by a piece of shrapnel. When we calculated the time difference, the plane had hit the *Tennessee* at the very time Mom and I were on our knees praying for Charles.

For the rest of her life, my mother joyed in the providence of God that miraculously delivered my brother. I saw her use that confidence in God to get her through many other tough times. She rested in the assurance that regardless of the circumstances, God is in control.

One of the greatest of God's gifts is personal peace. In our pressure-filled, fast-paced, technologically sophisticated world, personal peace is at a premium. The Bible predicted it would be so in the last days: "But you, Daniel, shut up the words, and seal the book until the time of the end; many shall run to and fro, and knowledge shall increase" (Daniel 12:4, *NKJV*).

One would think with all the modern conveniences, the time-saving devices, and the greatly increased knowledge, life would be much more peaceful and productive. The opposite seems to be true. Again, the Scriptures speak to this issue: "Then I applied myself to the understanding of wisdom, and also of madness and folly, but I learned that this, too, is a chasing after the wind. For with much wisdom comes much sorrow; the more knowledge, the more grief" (Ecclesiastes 1:17, 18). How ironic! The more we seek for worldly knowledge, the more frustrated we become. The more our own wisdom and knowledge increase, the more we suffer sorrow and grief. What a picture of contemporary society.

The Reality of Stress

Alvin Toffler, in his thought-provoking book, *Future Shock,* warns that the increasing rapid transition from an industrial to a super-technological society is stretching the adaptability of individuals beyond its limits. Add to these cultural developments the spiritual dimension where Satan is increasing his negative activities and you have a combination of factors that is physically, mentally and spiritually tough on the human machine. Stress-producing possibilities are everywhere.

Consequently, the number of people suffering from stress is increasing at a rapid rate. Christians are not exempt. What are some of the symptoms of stress that lead to "burnout"? Experts agree that the following factors persist in the life of a person who is a candidate for a serious mental breakdown:

• *Dissatisfaction* - A general discontent with what is happening in life

• *Restlessness* - Feeling the need to always be on the go, not content to settle down on a job, in a place of residence or in marriage

• *Persistent Fatigue* - Always tired, even after a night's sleep. Unable to benefit from time off

• *Irritability* - Easily upset, emotionally touchy, especially with family members, giving snap responses that are later regretted

• *Memory Lapse* - Consistently forgetful of important things, especially those related to interpersonal relationships

• *Frustration with Progress in Life* - Sense of overall failure, no hope for the future, dissatisfaction with past accomplishments

Occasionally, there may be a problem with biological inheritance or chemical imbalance over which a person has little or no control; but usually "burnout" or nervous collapse is the result of a violation of God's laws at the physical, mental, or spiritual level. The Bible makes it clear that it is God's will, despite situations or circumstances, for His people to experience personal peace—a calm assurance.

When Jesus talked openly with His disciples about the realities of life just before He went to the cross, He gave them this wonderful promise: "I am leaving you with a gift—peace of mind and heart. And the peace I give isn't like the peace the world gives. So don't be troubled or afraid" (John 14:27, *NLT*). There are many other Scriptural passages that picture His children as being emotionally stable and spiritually secure regardless of the storm that may be raging around them.

If this is true, then why do so many Christians find themselves depressed and discouraged instead of calm and confident? The answer is twofold: (1) there is a lack of knowledge and (2) there is a problem with obedience.

It is surprising how many Christians are ignorant of some of God's major truths, especially those relating to the everyday circumstances of life. So many of our difficulties stem directly from our ignorance of the very information that would resolve those dilemmas. In this regard, the Lord made a strong statement concerning Israel: "My people are destroyed from lack of knowledge" (Hosea 4:6). Unfortunately, the same could be said of many of God's children today.

On the other hand, we often find ourselves in trouble because we are unwilling to obey the laws we do know. The powerful combination of knowing the truth and putting it into practice will enable us to cope with any situation that may come our way. This ability to cope delivers us from the shackles of depression and gives us joy and peace in our life and relationships.

David wrote expressively about the ups and downs of life. In the Psalms he revealed his strong feelings about his problems with his enemies, his relationship with God, and what he perceived as the inequities in life. In spite of what sounds like a lot of complaining, David always came back to a balanced perspective and a positive outlook. A good example of this is found in Psalm 37. Here he talked about the realities of life, both positive and negative, then came to this bottom-line conclusion: "I was young and now I am old, yet I have never seen the righteous forsaken or their children begging bread" (v. 25).

The first part of Psalm 37 (vv. 1–8) lays down six basic truths about life. If these simple principles are followed, stress will be reduced and personal peace will be enhanced.

Don't Worry About Things You Can't Change

Much of our stress is brought about because we fret and worry about things—people and situations—we can't change. Three times in eight verses (vv. 1, 7, 8) we are told to stop worrying. As we mull over negative situations in our minds, depression envelopes us like a cloud. Nothing positive is accomplished by mental stewing. The derivation of the word *worry* is from Middle English and means "to choke, strangle, or constrict." That is what happens to our faith and our peace when we worry: they are choked to death.

We waste much valuable time and energy trying to change others. That is not possible. Besides, it is not our prerogative. We can change only one person—ourself. Since we are created as free moral agents, not even God can change us if we do not want to change. Why then do we fret so much about the behavior of others?

David says not to worry about evil men or those who do wrong. He tells us not to be concerned about those who succeed when they shouldn't, or become angry when wicked people get their way. We don't have the power or the right to control their attitudes and actions, even with those we love. What we can do is pray for others and live in such a way that we influence them positively. But we can't change them unless they want to be changed.

Norman Vincent Peale, author of *The Power of Positive Thinking* and pastor for many years of the Marble Collegiate Church in New York City, had many critics, but he always refused to strike back at them. When he was in his mid-80s and most of his critics had passed on, it was noted by one of his friends that Dr. Peale had not just outlived his critics, he had outloved them.

While we can't change other people, neither can we change many of the situations that cause us pain. We didn't cause them, and we can't make them go away. Death, disaster, disease, divorce—when these traumas crash in on us, we need all the physical, mental, and spiritual energies we can muster to cope with them. Being overly anxious and immersing ourself in worry can seriously deplete the reserves we need to survive.

The admonition to not worry about people or situations we can't change does not imply a denial of reality or a lack of concern. We recognize the problem, but we choose not to deal with it by worrying or fretting over it. When we do all we can, then we must leave the matter or the person in God's hands. We release our worry and anxiety to the Lord: "Let him have all your worries and cares, for he is always thinking about you and watching every-thing that concerns you" (1 Peter 5:7, TLB). If you want to have peace of mind and heart, don't worry about things you can't change.

Trust in the Lord and Do Good

God gives us a wonderful alternative to worrying. Instead of counting on our own resources to get us through, we can turn the matter over to Him. "Trust in the Lord and do good; dwell in the land and enjoy safe pasture" (Psalm 37:3). Trusting God, doing good, and being safe all go together. They follow one another in sequence. This principle brings us back to the central premise of this book. When we give priority to our relationship with God (trust in the Lord) and treat others as we should (do good), we will then be secure in life (dwell in the land and enjoy safe pasture).

The combination of trusting God and doing good is a powerful stress reducer. It shifts the focus away from our problems. Not only do we give the matter to God, but we go on from there to turn our attention to the needs of others. When Joseph was put in prison he trusted God to vindicate him, but he also ministered to those in prison with him. When Daniel was cast into the den of lions, he put his faith in God and continued his intercessory prayers. As Jesus was enduring the trauma of the cross, He trusted His Father; but He also had mercy on the thief and took care of the needs of His mother.

We know what glorious victories God gave Joseph, Daniel, and Jesus. In the midst of our own problems, if we follow the Scriptural pattern of trusting God and doing good, our deliverance also will be swift and sure.

> The fruit of righteousness will be peace; the effect of righteousness will be quietness and confidence forever. My people will live in peaceful dwelling places, in secure homes, in undisturbed places of rest. Though hail flattens the forest and the city is leveled completely, how blessed you will be, sowing your seed by every stream, and letting your cattle and donkeys range free (Isaiah 32:17-20, *NIV*).

Focus on yourself and your problems, and you will suffer great anxiety and stress. Trust in God and bless other people, and you will experience peace, confidence, and security.

Enjoy Your Life and Relationships

In Psalm 37:4 David gave another important principle concerning dealing with the pressures of life: "Delight yourself in the Lord and he will give you the desires of your heart." Rather than stewing in the juices of discontent and negativism, we are admonished to joy in our relationship with the Lord. It is important to note that this is more than a suggestion, it is in the form of an imperative. It is something we are to do, consciously and arbitrarily, regardless of the circumstances in which we find ourselves.

What does it mean to "delight yourself in the Lord"? Matthew Henry states that we are to joy in the "beauty, bounty, and benignity" of God. We need to think often of who God is and what He has done for us. We must learn to bask in His presence and revel in His goodness. We should squeeze all the good we can out of every positive relationship and from every good thing that happens to us. As we recount the blessings of God, we will sense a feeling of joy and happiness welling up within us. How much better to be lifted with joy from the Lord than to be burdened with discouragement from the devil. The choice is ours.

Commit Your Life to God

"Commit your way to the Lord; trust in him and he will do this: He will make your righteousness shine like the dawn, [and] the justice of your cause like the noonday sun" (Psalm 37:5, 6). Our problem with stress escalates when we try to fight our own battles and defend our own causes. One of the most difficult lessons for human beings to learn is that we can do only so much for ourselves. There comes a point when we must have help from God. It is so much better to understand that fact up front, rather than being forced to acknowledge it somewhere down the road.

The great benefit of committing our life to God and trusting in Him is that He will do for us what we cannot do for ourself. I can try to do good, but I cannot make myself righteous. Only God can do that. I can defend myself and explain my motives, but only God can vindicate me. How foolish for me to waste time and energy and get stressed out trying to do what God said He would do for me if only I would ask.

Rest in the Lord

Most of us have heard about the famous "contented" cows of evaporated milk notoriety. Growing up on a farm, I have often witnessed this picture of bovine serenity. Many times I have seen a cow, after she has eaten her fill of lush grass or sweet hay, circle an area to find the perfect place to lie down. When she finally settles on a spot and eases into a resting position, she assumes a look of total relaxation. She lazily closes her eyes and with obvious enjoyment slowly begins to chew her cud. She has become the contented cow.

David must have had that kind of contentment in mind when he wrote in Psalm 37:7, "Rest in the Lord, and wait patiently for Him" (NKJV). The frantic pace of our world does not lend itself to taking time for rest—spiritual or physical. The modern Christian has difficulty identifying with the imagery of Psalm 23: "He makes me lie down in green pastures, he leads me beside quiet waters" (v. 2). We don't have time even to eat a little spiritual food, let alone to stop and be quiet and wait patiently for the Lord. No wonder so many believers find themselves overcome by stress and anxiety.

Resting in the Lord involves making time for the spiritual disciplines of prayer, fasting, and reading and meditating on the Word of God. It means reordering priorities to put our relationship with God at the top of the list. Personal peace and contentment are not possible without adherence to this command.

Control Your Anger

David rounds out this important set of admonitions and promises in Psalm 37 by touching on one of the most vital of Scriptural principles: our responsibility to control our behavior. In this case, he zeros in on anger: "Refrain from anger and turn from wrath" (v. 8). Nothing can more quickly destroy our personal peace than unresolved anger.

Anger is a plague that devastates close relationships. It was the cause of the first murder. In our day it is at the heart of the violence that covers our land. In marriages and families it wreaks havoc. It is a mighty force that absolutely must be controlled.

We cannot avoid getting angry. It is a part of the human nature God gave us. It is how we handle anger that is important. We don't have to sin when we get angry. The Bible says, "If you are angry, don't sin by nursing your grudge. Don't let the sun go down with you still angry—get over it quickly" (Ephesians 4:26, *TLB*). That verse certainly implies that we have control over how we deal with our anger. Obeying God's command with regard to anger will ensure the peace of God in our heart.

The pattern given by David in Psalm 37, if it is followed, will strengthen our self-image and bring a calm assurance to our spirits. Use it as a checklist for your own life:

• Are you worrying about things you can't change?

- Are you trusting in the Lord and trying to do good?
- Are you enjoying your life and your relationships?
- Have you committed your life to God?
- Are you trying to rest in the Lord?
- Are you controlling your anger?

CHAPTER 13

A. Quiet Confidence

We come to the final chapter of this book, completing the cycle of God's order for relationships: loving God, loving others, loving ourself. As we finish talking about the principle of loving ourselves, we arrive at the point where we began and where we must always begin—loving God with all our heart, with all our soul, with all our mind, and with all our strength. Understanding and practicing God's order and balance in relationship brings a sense of wholeness and fulfillment that ultimately produces in us an "inexpressible and glorious joy" (1 Peter 1:8). This is God's will for our life.

In the book *The Practice of Christian Perfection: Crucified Love*, Robin Maas makes this statement: "The first effect of the arrival of love in our lives is to give us an entirely new image of ourselves (we must be wonderful, because someone wonderful loves us)"

(p. 59). The Bible says, "Therefore, if anyone is in Christ, he is a new creation; the old has gone, the new has come!" (2 Corinthians 5:17). When we first come to Christ, and before we understand fully what it means to love God and to love others, God begins to re-create and restore our self-image which has been marred by the effects of sin. In my life, this began to happen at an early age.

When I was 8 years old, things were not going well in my world. My mom and dad were separated and on the verge of divorce. My mom, my younger sister, three older brothers and I were living in California in dire poverty. We were existing, literally, from hand to mouth. Dad was gone, having hitchhiked to New York City on the promise of a job. I had never gone to church, never prayed, never read the Bible. I was totally unaware of the wonderful Christian heritage our family had—a heritage my parents, at that point in their lives, had chosen to reject.

One Sunday morning I was playing in our front yard when I noticed a bus from the local Nazarene church drive by our house. I had seen that bus before, but on this morning the idea struck me to ride that bus to church the next Sunday. Mom wasn't too enthusiastic about the idea at first, but she finally gave her consent.

The next Sunday morning I was waiting as the bus came around the corner. I flagged it down. The driver pulled over and opened the door. "What can I do for you, Son?" he asked. I told him I would like to go to church. "That's what we're here for. Jump on board." Thus began an adventure that would completely change my life. A loving God was directing the steps of a little boy who knew nothing at all about Him.

When we arrived at church, they took me to a small classroom in the basement where there were a few other kids my age, but nobody I knew. There, for the first time in my life, I heard the story of Jesus. I went back the next Sunday; and at the end of the class, the teacher asked if there was anyone who would like to accept Jesus as Savior. I didn't really understand what I was doing, but I raised my hand. The teacher had me kneel beside my chair and repeat a prayer after her. Something happened in my heart. When I got home that day, I ran to tell my mom what had happened. As I excitedly told her the story, to my dismay, she started to cry. I asked her if I had done something wrong. "Oh, no, Son," she said, brushing aside her tears. "What you did was wonderful. Mommy's happy for you."

I found out later she wrote my dad that very day and asked him to come home. She told him I had become a Christian and that she wanted to get her life and their marriage straightened out. A few weeks later, without anyone knowing he was coming, my dad walked back into our lives. To my great delight, the next Sunday morning he rode the bus with me to church. As the pastor preached during the morning worship service, my dad began to shake and cry. I didn't know what was going on. When the invitation was given, Dad rushed forward and fell in the altar. God was performing miracles in my family.

The following Sunday I thought my heart was going to burst with joy as my mom and my little sister joined Dad and me on the bus. A few Sundays later, Mom recommitted her life to the Lord. Other good things started happening in our family, and I began to understand the personal nature of a loving God. It blew my mind that He knew who I was and that He cared about what was going on in my life. His love made me know how valuable I was as a person. What God had done in my life and in my family gave me a confidence in Him and in myself that has stayed with me through the years. "Being confident of this, that he who began a good work in you will carry it on to completion until the day of Christ Jesus" (Philippians 1:6).

The story of Gideon is an excellent example of the contrast between the way God sees us and the way we see ourselves. Out of their beclouded life perspective and with help from the devil, most people have an inner sense of inferiority and a lack of self-confidence. When an angel called Gideon a "mighty man of valor," his reply was, "But Lord . . . how can I save Israel? My clan is the weakest in Manasseh, and I am the least in my family" (see Judges 6:12, 15, 16). The angel ignored Gideon's negative response and again gave him God's perspective: "I will be with you, and you will strike down all the Midianites together [as if they were but one man]" (v. 16).

Gideon's attitude is too common among believers, even though the promise of God is staring them in the face. We are greatly impacted by the devil's persistent message. His message is always negative or has negative implications. God's message to His children is always positive or has positive implications.

The devil puts us down; God lifts us up.

The devil condemns us; God forgives us.

The devil accuses us; God encourages us.

The devil binds us; God sets us free!

The devil will tell you you're ugly, weak, defeated, sinful, a loser. God says you're beautiful, strong, victorious, redeemed, a winner!

I was speaking at a singles conference when the Lord stopped me in the middle of my message and gave me a special word for the congregation. Here is what I sensed the Lord saying: "If you ever hear any wounding, condemning, judgmental words, they don't come from Me; they come from your enemy, the devil."

Someone might ask, "But what about when I sin, when I'm disobedient, or when I fail?" When we do wrong, God will convict us and perhaps even chastise us, but He will never wound us or condemn us. As long as we ask Him, He will forgive us, have mercy on us, and strengthen us; but He will not judge us until that day when the door of mercy is finally closed.

We should understand, as the devil does, that when we suffer from a poor self-image and we lack self-confidence, we are never able to reach our potential and accomplish God's purpose for our life. Gideon could never have defeated the Midianites if he had not become convinced that with God's help he could live up to the name God gave him: *a mighty man of valor*. Satan will do his best to debilitate, distract, disillusion, discourage, and depress you. His ultimate aim is to destroy you. He knows that low self-esteem leads to ruinous behavior—drugs, sexual perversion, mental illness, suicide.

Despite his initial doubts and his testing of God's word, Gideon did come to believe that God meant what He said. He learned to trust in God and not in human wisdom or the strength of armies. He became a mighty warrior and an inspirational leader. God used him to deliver His people. The process he went through to reach that point is instructive for us today.

Understand Who You Are

Gideon's confidence grew strong when he finally came to understand who he was. In the beginning, he saw himself as a "nobody." He disparaged both himself and his family. He was negative about his people and doubted God's concern for them: "If the Lord is with us, why has all this happened to us? Where are all his wonders that our fathers told us about when they said, 'Did not the Lord bring us up out of Egypt?' But now the Lord has abandoned us and put us into the hand of Midian" (Judges 6:13).

It is detrimental to us and displeasing to God when we talk negatively about ourself. When we put ourself down, we are disparaging God's creation, and even worse, we are talking badly about one of God's children. When we behave this way we disillusion other people, especially those closest to us. We make the grace and power of God of no effect in our life.

Often, such negative remarks are calculated to elicit sympathy or a counter- statement. In those cases, we are guilty of false humility. Whatever a person's motivation for saying negative things about himself, he is violating God's Word and needs to ask God's forgiveness. The only time a believer has permission to make self-condemning statements is as an act of repentance (Psalm 51) or to show the contrast between human and the divine (Romans 7). We should not be guilty of Gideon's mistake.

Only when Gideon became convinced of the validity of God's promise was he able to change his view of himself. When he finally understood that God was with him, he began to believe he could accomplish what God had told him to do. He gained confidence that he was favored and chosen of God. He began to feel the hand of God upon him.

That was the secret of David's success. Standing before Goliath, he remembered God's anointing when he killed the lion and the bear. Paul referred many times to his Damascus- road experience.

We must remind ourselves again and again of the promises He has made to us personally. We must recall what God has done for us in the past. We are children of God. We are the apple of His eye. We can do all things through Christ who strengthens us (Philippians 4:13).

On the other hand, we can never forget that we are frail human beings. In our own power and wisdom, we can do little. We will ultimately fail. We are subject to temptation and we are often a captive of our feelings. We must constantly fight the tendency to trust in the arm of flesh because the flesh is weak and corruptible. *The Amplified Bible's* rendering of Proverbs 3:5- 8 gives wonderful insight into the ongoing battle to keep fleshly attitudes and ambitions in place:

> Lean on, trust in, and be confident in the Lord with all your heart and mind and do not rely on your own insight or understanding. In all your ways know, recognize, and acknowledge Him, and He will direct and make straight and plain your paths. Be not wise in your own eyes; reverently fear and worship the Lord and turn [entirely] away from evil. It shall be health to your nerves and sinews, and marrow and moistening to your bones.

When Gideon plugged into the divine formula, he moved quickly from self-doubt to self-assurance. He was able to turn his fear into faith and his defeat into victory. The Lord literally transformed a weak, insecure, intimidated child of God into a mighty man of valor. He went from "the least among his brothers" to a leader of God's people. The path Gideon followed is the same one we must travel if we are to become confident in the Lord and accomplish feats for Him.

Get Rid of the Idols in Your Life

Before God could use Gideon in defeating the Midianites, he had to tear down the altar of Baal and destroy the Asherah pole which the Israelites had been using for worship in defiance of Jehovah. Not only did Gideon destroy these places of idol worship, but he used the wood from those altars to present a sacrifice to the Lord (see Judges 6:25-27). It was not enough to stop worshiping the idols, but true worship had to be reinstituted.

While the idols of Gideon's day kept Israel in bondage, the same is true of God's people today. An idol is a representation or symbol of an object of worship. The problem is that the symbol becomes more than a representation; it becomes a god in itself—a false god. This is why Jehovah commanded, "Do not make idols or set up an image or a sacred stone for yourselves, and do not place a carved stone in your land to bow down before it. I am the Lord your God" (Leviticus 26:1). Many of the idols in Israel began as symbols representing Jehovah. The idea was that the people would worship God through the image, but soon the image became an idol. In common terms, an idol is a substitute for the real thing, an object of misplaced devotion. God says all such images and symbols must go.

In modern society, especially in the contemporary church, we do not have much problem with graven images or carved stones becoming our gods. But we do have a great deal of trouble with idols—substitutes, obsessions, objects of misplaced devotion. Anything that usurps the place of God in our lives, that keeps us from giving our total self to God in true worship, is an idol. Any obsession that has a hold on us, that we in essence bow down to—whether money, pride, sex, career, fame, clothes, perfectionism—

comes between us and God and makes a loving relationship with Him impossible. The Bible characterizes idolatry as an adulterous relationship.

Continuing the story of Gideon, the Bible tells how the gifts of gold that were given to honor Gideon for defeating the Midianites became a stumbling block to Israel: "Gideon made the gold into an ephod, which he placed in Ophrah, his town. All Israel prostituted themselves by worshiping it there, and it became a snare to Gideon and his family" (Judges 8:27). What a lesson for the church today! How many "golden ephods" have caused some of God's people to prostitute themselves in idolatrous worship?

The bottom line about the worship of idols is that a Christian cannot have confidence in his relationship with God or in himself when he knows he is not being true to his spiritual commitment. His adulterous behavior will betray him.

What do idols do to our relationship with God?

First of all, they create a distraction. They cause us to take our eyes off of the Bridegroom. They divert our attention.

Second, they create a false trust. We begin to look to the idol to meet our needs and satisfy our desires.

Third, they divide our affection. We cannot serve two masters. We cannot swear two allegiances. Every idol, every obsession, every addiction, every substitute must be removed from our life. In the end, only the time, energy, and commitment we put into our relationship with God will count toward our eternal destiny. Only as we strengthen our spiritual relationship will we gain the personal confidence to do exploits for God.

Turn your eyes upon Jesus,
 Look full in His wonderful face,

And the things of earth will grow strangely dim
In the light of His glory and grace.

Depend Upon God as Your Resource

When Gideon understood who he was in the Lord and got rid of the idols in his life, he was ready to fight the Midianites with rising faith and confidence. This was quite a change from his initial timid response. The steps he took transformed his entire outlook. Now he was eager for a confrontation with the enemy. He was really beginning to feel like a mighty man of valor. But he had one more lesson to learn.

Gideon got so bold with the anointing of God upon him that he blew the trumpet to summon the armies of Israel. Would anyone respond to this man who only a short time before called himself "the least in my father's house"? To his amazement, over 30,000 volunteers showed up. Now he was a general. He was beginning to like this job. His new troops were "gung ho" and he was sure he had the right battle plan.

But God had a different idea.

God began to take away Gideon's resources. He whittled the army down from 32,000 to 300. It seemed like such an unreasonable thing. But, as always, God had the best interests of His people in mind. He did not want them to trust in the arm of flesh. "The Lord said to Gideon, 'You have too many warriors with you. If I let all of you fight the Midianites, the Israelites will boast to me that they saved themselves by their own strength'" (Judges 7:2, NLT).

God loves us too much to allow us to get "too big for our britches." That may happen, but it will be in disregard of God's repeated warnings. This is a subject that God feels strongly about. In fact, He pronounces judgment on those who rely on resources other than His. God does not want us trafficking with strangers and foreigners. It's not good for the relationship. We have to love God and Him alone; we have to depend on Him for our resources. Isaiah warned, "Woe to those who go down to Egypt for help, who rely on horses, who trust in the multitude of their chariots and in the great strength of their horsemen, but do not look to the Holy One of Israel, or seek help from the Lord" (31:1).

Because Gideon listened to the Lord and obeyed His commands, he was used of God to defeat the Midianites and in doing so made his mark on history. He is one of the few Old Testament characters mentioned in the New Testament. Not bad for a farm boy with a supersized inferiority complex! The pattern he followed is not difficult to discern. Take note one more time:

- He understood who he really was in the Lord.
- He got rid of the idols in his life.
- He depended on God as his resource.

God is telling us to go and do likewise!

Epilogue

Writing this book has been a difficult but reinforcing experience for me. I struggled at times, wondering if I was doing an adequate job of putting into words the all-important principles on which this book is based. Several times during the course of the writing I stopped and asked myself if my words were conveying these vital Scriptural truths in a relevant way. Despite my desire and effort and even with the reviews and rewritings, I'm sure I fell far short of the mark in several areas.

While recognizing my inadequacy to express on paper what I feel in my heart, I must say that this writing experience has been exhilarating because it has reinforced my strong conviction about the priority of relationship. I did not intend to be as autobiographical as I have been, but the more I wrote, the more examples from my own life came to mind. I began to realize that these ideas have been a part of me and developing in me for a lifetime.

The message of this book is actually threefold: the *centrality*, the *order*, and the *joy* of relationship. The first two are so Scripturally important that Jesus embodied them in what is called the Great Commandment or, as we have termed it, "God's most important message to man." The third aspect, the *joy* of relationship, is a precious gift from God that makes the first two parts of the message meaningful and complete. It must be said again, at the end of this book, as it was at the beginning, "God intends all relationships to be joyful."

If this threefold message is understood and appropriated in the life of a believer, it will bring God's blessings of fulfillment and happiness. Like other divine laws, it is a two-edged sword. If it is obeyed, it carries great rewards; if disobeyed, dire consequences ensue. No doubt much of what is wrong in the world today is a result of the violation of this greatest of all commandments: "Love the Lord your God with all your heart . . . soul . . . strength . . . mind, and, Love your neighbor as yourself" (Luke 10:27).

The consistency of this law of God is seen in so many aspects of life. The chart on the following page shows how the order of *God, others, self* applies at other levels.

A Diagram of Scriptural Relationships
Always moving from left to right

PERSONS	God	⟹ Others	⟹ Self
DIRECTION	Upward	⟹ Outward	⟹ Inward
BEHAVIOR	Being	⟹ Doing	⟹ Feeling
EMPHASIS	Word	⟹ Fruit	⟹ Joy
RESULT	Character	⟹ Caring	⟹ Confidence

You will notice that in every area on the chart the beginning source is God. Everything flows from our relationship with God. That flow continues through our relationship with others and finally to our relationship with ourself. Once that relationship cycle is complete, it begins again, moving from self back to God. When we are in right relationship with God, we will be in a position to relate properly to others. Good relationships with God and others build a strong self-image. A strong self-image enhances our relationship with God. And so the cycle continues, strengthening relationships at all three levels each time the pattern is followed.

One further point of explanation: Each time we come into right relationship with God and with others, we are changed for the better. With God as our source, we are able to bear good fruit that will bless and nourish others, which in turn will give us a sense of fulfillment and satisfaction. When the right relationship order is followed, the self is immediately impacted in a positive way. We do not begin with self, we begin with God.

Study Questions

he following questions can be used as an aid in personal study or as a stimulus for group discussion. It is always helpful to write out the answers, especially in personal study.

CHAPTER 1 · The Priority of Relationship

1. Give your own definition of the word *relationship*.

2. Read again the Ten Commandments in Exodus 20:1-17. How does each commandment relate to God? to others? to self?

3. List three practical ways of focusing on the vertical relationship with God.

4. What are some of the results of the "self-first" philosophy in society? in church? in marriage and family?

5. Think of a relationship problem you face in your life at this moment. What should be your approach or behavior to this problem in light of the Scriptural order of God, others, self?

CHAPTER 2 · The Power of Joy

1. Name two ways grief can be turned into joy.

2. Who are three people you remember with joy? Think of a particular happening that brought you joy in your relationship with each of those persons.

3. List three things you can do with joy to counter the opposition of enemies.

4. Interpret the statement: "The smallest package I have ever seen is a man wrapped up in himself?"

5. How can we refer to "I" without being proud or egotistical?

CHAPTER 3 · Centering Your Affection

1. What things in your life tend to distract you from focusing on your relationship with God first? Think of practical ways to put those things in their proper place.

2. What comes to mind when you think of your "first love" for Christ? How has that changed in comparison to your relationship with the Lord today?

3. Why do you think God says we should love him first with our heart—that is, our emotion and devotion?

4. Name two dangers in spiritual manifestations. How can those dangers be avoided?

5. Read Isaiah 58. Why didn't God accept the religious practices of the people? What did He tell them they must do to change? What rewards did He promise them if they would change?

CHAPTER 4 · Giving Your Life

1. Explain this statement: "Spiritual complacency is the worst form of blasphemy?"

2. How can we maintain strong personal convictions without becoming judgmental of others? (See Romans 14.)

3. How does the current trend against commitment manifest itself in your own life? in your family? in your church?

4. Read Revelation 3:14-22. Name three ways the church today can be compared to the church at Laodicea.

5. What is the spiritual significance of "building a new altar" as Jacob did at Bethel?

CHAPTER 5 · Setting Your Mind

1. Why is the transformation of the mind, in the spiritual sense, so important?

2. What do you consider the three major problems in contemporary society? How have these problems affected the church?

3. God not only sanctifies our thoughts, He also sensitizes them. What is difference?

4. Why does the ability to choose imply accountability?

5. Identify two areas in your own life where you need to love God more in your mind (thinking).

CHAPTER 6 · Practicing Your Worship

1. How should disagreements over worship styles be handled?

2. Give two reasons why the remembering of the blessings of God is so important.

3. How would you define growth in worship?

4. List two ways to extend worship to everyday living.

5. Interpret the statement: "Every person we come in contact with is a test of our relationship with God?"

CHAPTER 7 · The Heart of the Message

1. List four principles of interpersonal relationships that Jesus demonstrated in His encounter with the woman at the well. Apply each to a present relationship in your life.

2. Give three examples of Jesus' behavior in which He confronted people.

3. What does the Bible say is the connection between loving God and loving others?

4. What are the implications of the concept that ministry to others begins with our family members?

5. How can God judge us in our relationships with others when we have no control over their behavior?

CHAPTER 8 · The Attitude of Joy

1. How can we use the powerful impact our behavior has on others to positive advantage?

2. Why are family relationships some of the most important and impact us most?

3. What are some things we can do to make our relationships with others joyful?

4. What are the three elements of Paul's formula for relationship with friends?

5. What is the primary source of joy in relationships with foes? Why is this source so important?

CHAPTER 9 · The Law of Fruitbearing

1. Explain this statement: "The quality of our relationships is determined by the fruit we bear."

2. List ten "good" and ten "bad" spiritual fruits.

3. According to the author there is essentially no "private" behavior. What does this mean?

4. What is the ultimate test of the character (goodness or badness) of our spiritual fruit?

5. In general, how has society tried to get rid of "bad fruit"? What is the best way to accomplish this?

CHAPTER 10 · The Healing of Relationships

1. Give three reasons for Joseph's success in life.

2. What is the only control we have in situations where people build walls of negative behavior?

3. List the three types of spiritual walls people build.

4. Explain this statement: "When we understand that God is sovereign in our lives, we will not be so quick to blame others for the bad things that happen to us."

5. What threefold pattern did Joseph use to bring about reconciliation with his brothers?

CHAPTER 11 · The Apple of His Eye

1. How has secular humanism inverted God's order of relationship?

2. Why does God want our self-esteem to be high?

3. What is the greatest reason so many people have feelings of inferiority?

4. Think of at least three instances in the past year that prove God's concern for you. Review each situation and let joy and praise flow in your heart.

5. What is the purpose of God making promises to his children?

CHAPTER 12 · A Calm Assurance

1. List six characteristics of stress that can lead to burnout or mental breakdown. Use these as a checklist in your own life.

2. Give the two reasons some Christians find themselves depressed and discouraged.

3. What is wrong with worry?

4. What does it mean to "delight yourself in the Lord?"

5. In what ways does the Scripture say we are to control our anger?

CHAPTER 13 · A Quiet Confidence

1. What was God's purpose in calling Gideon a "mighty man of valor?"

2. Give three reasons it is wrong to put ourselves down.

3. Name some examples of modern idols. How should these things be dealt with?

4. List three ways idols negatively impact our relationship with God?

5. Why did God take away Gideon's resources, and why does He sometimes do the same with us?